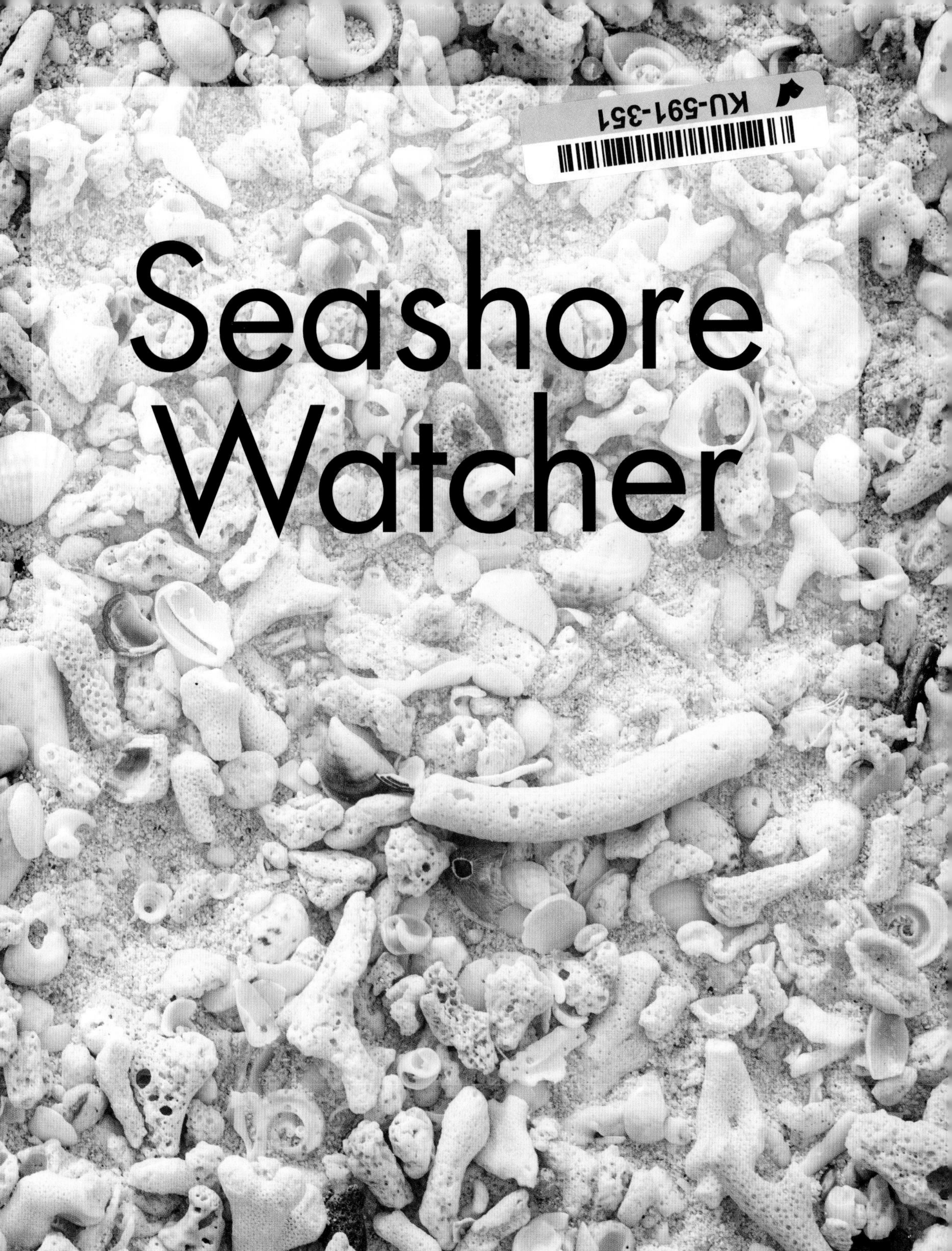

Seashore Watcher

Quarto is the authority on a wide range of topics.
Quarto educates, entertains and enriches the lives of our readers—enthusiasts and lovers of hands-on living.
www.quartoknows.com

Author: Maya Plass
Design: Mike Henson and Cloud King Creative
Editorial: Emily Stead and Emily Pither

First Published in 2018 **by QED Publishing,
an imprint of The Quarto Group.
The Old Brewery,** 6 **Blundell Street,
London** N7 9BH, **United Kingdom.**
T (0)20 7700 6700 F (0)20 7700 8066
www.QuartoKnows.com

A catalogue record for this book is available from the British Library.

ISBN 978 1 78493 870 3

Manufactured in Dongguan, China TL112017

9 8 7 6 5 4 3 2 1

The words in **BOLD** are explained in the Glossary on page 112.

Seashore
Watcher

Maya Plass

QED

Contents

The seashore

A seashore is where the sea meets the land. It is a tough environment, where only the most hardy animals and plants survive. The tides roll in and out, as the seas are pulled by the moon's gravity. Each day, at high tide, the sea covers the shore. Then at low tide, the sea flows back out, uncovering rocks and sand. Animals and plants must be able to live in both cold waters and sunshine.

Hardy barnacles

Spiky sea urchins

Super seashores

At almost 250 km long, the sandy seashore of Praia do Cassino in Brazil is the longest beach in the world. Meanwhile, Australia has the second-longest beach: Ninety Mile Beach, as its name suggests, measures a whopping 90 miles (145 km). Padre Island National Seashore, in the US state of Texas, also has an impressive shoreline that covers over 110 km.

THE UPPER SHORE

The best time to explore the seashore is when the tide is out.

Seashore zones

The seashore is made up of different **zones**:

- The splash zone: Where the rocks at the top of the beach are sprayed with salty water.
- The upper zone: Above the high-tide mark, snails and seaweed species, which can live out of water for long periods, can be found here.
- The middle shore: Between the high and low tides, barnacles and limpets keep themselves moist here until the sea covers them once again.
- The lower shore: Only seen at the lowest of tides, here we find beautiful marine creatures like starfish and sea urchins.

THE LOWER ZONE

THE MIDDLE SHORE

Seashore safety

- Seaweed-covered rocks can be slippery. Take care when exploring the seashore.

Did you know?

Around 8000 years ago, a huge tsunami hit the United Kingdom and turned it in to an island. Low-lying land that connected the UK with Europe became flooded, creating what is now called the North Sea and the English Channel.

Be a seashore watcher

Low tides are great for spotting all sorts of marine wildlife. Even on the high tide you will discover treasures such as seaweed and shells washed up on the beach. Seals, dolphins and sea birds can often be spotted not far from the shore without binoculars.

Spotting seals in Big Sur, California, USA.

Rock pools can be packed with beach treasures.

Finding wildlife

Seashore creatures will hear you coming, and feel your footsteps vibrate through the rocks, so tread gently and quietly.

- When you arrive, check that the beach is safe, then identify the best places to explore.
- Take a bucket to collect beach treasures, then examine your prizes.
- If you are exploring a rocky shore, look under rocks, seaweed and in crevices, but don't forget to follow the Seashore Code (you'll find this on pages 12–13).
- Look closely at any creatures you find. Try to guess how they might move, feed or breathe.

A seashore watcher's top tips

- Ask local people which are the best beaches for wildlife watching, then get to know one beach well.
- Walk quietly, then choose a comfortable spot and remain still to improve your chances of a wildlife encounter.
- Draw pictures of anything you don't recognise to look up later.

Did you know?

If you visit a beach the morning after strong storms and big waves, you may spot some rare marine creatures that have washed onto the shore.

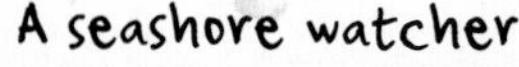

A seashore watcher

Alien-like goose barnacles cling to driftwood.

Seashore safety

- Check the weather and tides before you leave the house.
- Make sure an adult knows where you are at all times.
- Remember, seaweed on rocks can be slippery, so tread carefully.

Seashore-watcher essentials

To make the most of your seashore experience, remember to take great care, and keep your eyes and ears open. The right footwear and clothing are important to avoid injury, sunburn or **hypothermia**.

Seashore-watcher kit

Here are some useful bits of kit to pack. Don't worry if you don't have all these things, you'll still have a great day out.

- bucket
- clear plastic pots
- magnifying glass
- notebook
- pencil
- seashore guide
- binoculars
- camera (with secure wrist or shoulder strap to avoid saltwater dunking).
- rucksack, for your kit, and to keep your hands free while exploring rocky areas.

Exploring the seashore at sunset.

What to wear?

You can enjoy exploring the seashore in almost any weather. Here's what to wear on your trip:

- Wellies, boots or sturdy shoes with a good grip that you don't mind getting wet.
- Sun cream, long sleeves and hats for hot, sunny days.
- Layers and waterproofs for chillier, rainy days.

Wet-weather clothing

Seashore safety

- If you see something sharp or dangerous, leave it where it is and tell an adult.
- Avoid touching jellyfish – those washed onto the shore may still sting!
- Read public-information signs on the beach for useful information.

A sign at Surfers Corner, near Cape Town, South Africa.

The Seashore Code

The Seashore Code tells us how to stay safe at the coast and enjoy the wildlife that lives there, without causing any harm. If we all 'take only photographs and leave only footprints', we will make sure that our seashores remain beautiful and full of life for years to come.

Exploring the rocky shore

All seashore watchers should remember these important things:

- put rocks back in the same place as you found them. This will give animals shelter from the heat of the sun as well as predators;
- don't pull seaweed from the rocks. It's home to all sorts of creatures;
- don't kick or remove limpets from the rocks;
- never poke soft creatures like **anemones**;
- handle animals with care and observe in clear pots with a little fresh seawater;
- return animals to where you found them;
- wash your hands before eating anything and after your adventure.

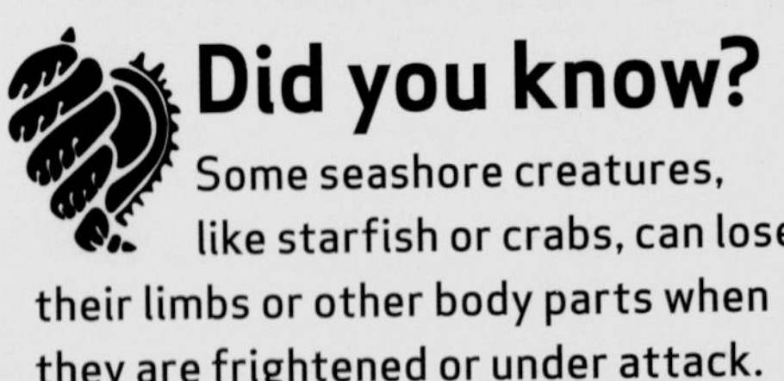

Did you know?

Some seashore creatures, like starfish or crabs, can lose their limbs or other body parts when they are frightened or under attack.

What will you uncover in a rock pool?

It can take up to a year for a starfish to regrow a lost limb.

Seashore safety

- Take litter home with you.
- Leave shells and creatures on the beach.
- Keep away from quicksand and soft mud.
- Stay away from dangerous cliffs.

Pay attention to warning signs on your visit.

Litter can cause harm to wildlife.

Watching seashore wildlife

When watching wildlife at the seashore, remember to:

- give sea birds plenty of space to nest and look after their young;
- stay clear of seals resting on the beach;
- do not disturb wild animals – give them the time and space to feed and play.

Watch wildlife from a distance using binoculars.

Checking the tides

The tides shape the seashore and create a very special environment. Creatures that live between the tides are suited to living both in and out of the water. Learning about the tides will help you to find the best tidal pools.

Starfish in a shallow tide pool.

TIDAL INFORMATION		
Date	Tues 12th Aug	
High Water	13:00	9.8 m
Low Water	20:00	0.5 m
Wind	SW	20 mph
Conditions	Rough	
Sea Temp.	17°c	
Air Temp.	16°c	

Tidal information can be found on beach displays.

What causes the tides?

The tides are created by the gravitational pull of the moon and the sun. The pull is at its strongest when the moon and sun are in line with the earth, when the moon is full or new.

Tide tables

A local tide table or display panel will tell you the time of the high and low tides. Most seashores around the world will have two high and two low tides. Tidal information will usually tell you:

- the date;
- the time of the high tide (or high water);
- the height of the high tide – the higher this number, the less beach there is;
- the time of the low tide;
- the height of the low tide – the lower this number, the more seashore there is to explore.

Spring and neap tides

Spring tides are when there are very-low low tides and very-high high tides. These happen at full and new moons. The tides rise and fall quickest on spring tides.

Neap tides happen at the first or last quarter phases of the moon. The difference between the high tide and the low tide is at its smallest. The tides rise and fall more slowly on a neap tide.

Tide top tips

- Follow the tide out as it drops, and head back to high shore before the tide turns.
- Head to the seashore during the low tides of spring tides, when the lower shore can be explored, revealing many delicate species.

Neap tide at Morston Creek, Norfolk, UK.

Did you know?

The biggest tides are found in Canada in the Bay of Fundy, which separates New Brunswick from Nova Scotia. Here, the difference between the high and the low tide is a massive 16.3 metres.

Hopewell Rocks, in the Bay of Fundy, on the high and low tides.

Seashore safety

- The tide can change very quickly. Keep an eye on the time and the changing tide to avoid becoming stranded.

Checking the weather

The weather can change quickly at the coast, so it's important to check the weather forecast on the morning of your trip, before setting out. This will help you plan your clothing and keep you safe at the seashore. Some weather conditions are only suitable for the toughest of barnacles!

Seashore safety

- Avoid the water's edge and stand well back from big waves.
- Head for home if a heavy storm is forecast.
- Never take risks when taking photographs.
- Heavy rain and long dry periods can make cliffs unstable.

Dangerous waves at Portreath, on the Cornish coast, UK.

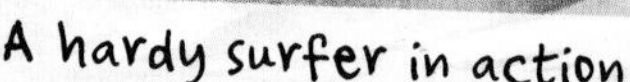

A hardy surfer in action

A tropical storm at Miami Beach, Florida, USA.

Did you know?

Hurricanes form over tropical oceans. The oceans shape our weather and our climate, both at sea and on land – even areas hundreds of miles away from any coastline.

Solar power

Don't forget your sun cream and hat. The power of the sun's ultra-violet (UV) radiation can easily burn our skin.

UV radiation is strongest:

- around midday when the sun's rays are most direct;
- closest to the equator where the sun's rays travel the least distance to the earth from the sun;
- when reflected off sand and sea foam;
- when there is only light cloud.

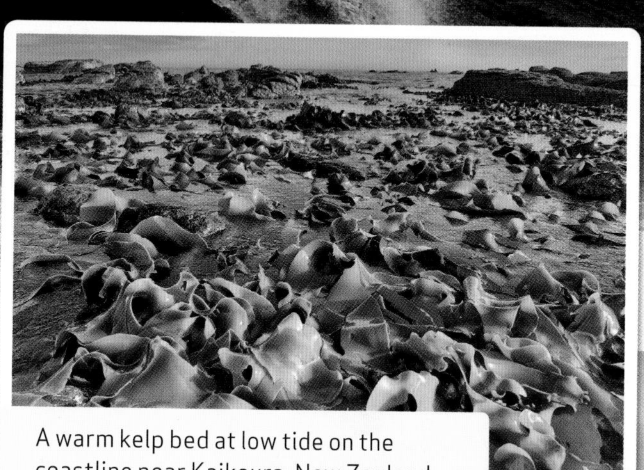

A warm kelp bed at low tide on the coastline near Kaikoura, New Zealand.

Sand reflects the sun's rays and makes them stronger.

Fun fact

On a summer's day in New Zealand at high tide the water may be as cool as 10°C, but at low tide the pools can be heated by the sun to as hot as 40°C.

Keeping a nature journal

Keeping a seashore watcher's notebook and pencil at hand will help you record what you have seen, how you felt and remember questions that you may have.

What to include?

The following information can help keep your notes in order:

- date
- times of day
- weather
- area of seashore explored
- times of low and high tides
- heights of low and high tides
- interesting facts
- sketches

A journal will keep your seashore memories safe for years to come.

Keeping notes on creatures

You can begin to understand more about the wildlife you see by taking notes, making observations and asking questions. You might:

- draw a sketch of a creature;
- note where you saw it;
- write what the creature was doing;
- think of questions to answer later.

Sit quietly, make observations and take notes.

How to record what you find

- place your creature in a bucket or pot, then take some time to observe it;
- look closely – from every angle and in great detail;
- study the different colours;
- carefully, use your hands to feel how hard, soft, furry or slimy your creature is;
- sketch a rough drawing of your creature first; then add more detail to your picture;
- take photos to allow you to finish your drawings at home.

Use a small pot to observe animals.

Saving Our Seashores (SOS)

Our seashores can give us lots of happy memories and experiences. There are a few simple things that we can do to help protect our seashores, so that we can continue to enjoy them in the future.

Human impact

It is important that we look after our seas. They give us water, food, medicine, oxygen to breathe, and even help regulate our climate. Overfishing and pollution have become major threats to the health of our oceans. Using too many fossil fuels causes sea levels to rise and changes in sea temperature, too.

A guillemot is cleaned after being polluted by oil.

Help to tidy up a beach near you.

SOS… on your visit

- take only photographs, leave only footprints;
- always bring your litter home with you;
- join local beach cleans and recycle the rubbish you find;
- follow the Seashore Code (turn back to pages 12–13).

SOS… from home

- eat fish that is sustainably caught (in ways that reduce damage caused to the environment);
- reduce the electricity that you use to help stop the warming of our oceans;
- never put chemicals, baby wipes, cotton buds or plastic down the sink or toilet.

Try to save energy at home.

SOS… at school

- take your nature journal to school to share your discoveries;
- encourage your school to help you learn about the seashore;
- think of three things that could be done at school to help reduce litter or pollution at sea;
- get involved in World Oceans Day on the 8th of June each year;
- remind your teachers and friends of fantastic sea facts.

Did you know?

Most of the earth's oxygen we need to breathe comes from tiny ocean plants called plankton.

Even a five-minute beach clean can help to save wildlife.

Beach cleans

Beach litter endangers hundreds of marine species, from whales and sea birds to tiny plankton that eat or become tangled in dangerous rubbish. Beach cleans keep our beaches safe and looking good. They protect marine life, and being involved can be very rewarding.

Beach-clean kit

We can help to clean our beaches every time we visit the seashore, or as part of a larger, organised group event. Here are some things you'll need to join a beach clean.

- protective gloves
- bin bags
- sturdy footwear
- tub for adults to put sharp objects in

Volunteers cleaning up on Nha Trang, one of Vietnam's most beautiful beaches.

What might I find?

- balloons
- plastic bags, bottles and lids
- cigarette stubs
- small pieces of plastic
- fishing line and nets
- cotton buds
- mermaids' tears (Read about these on pages 24–25.)

Ghost nets are fishing nets that have been left or lost in the ocean by fishermen. They continue to catch fish for hundreds of years.

Where does marine litter come from?

By recording types of beach litter collected at clean-ups, we can tell which are the main causes of litter:

- public waste like litter left on the beach or washed down drains and waterways;
- fishing waste like old lobster pots or nets lost in storms;
- sewage-related debris, like baby wipes or cotton buds;
- shipping waste like items thrown overboard;
- medical waste like syringes.

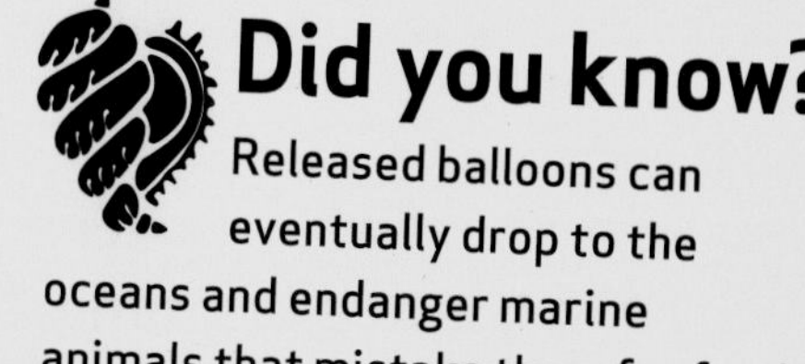

Did you know?

Released balloons can eventually drop to the oceans and endanger marine animals that mistake them for food.

Deflated balloons can become blocked in the stomachs of birds and animals.

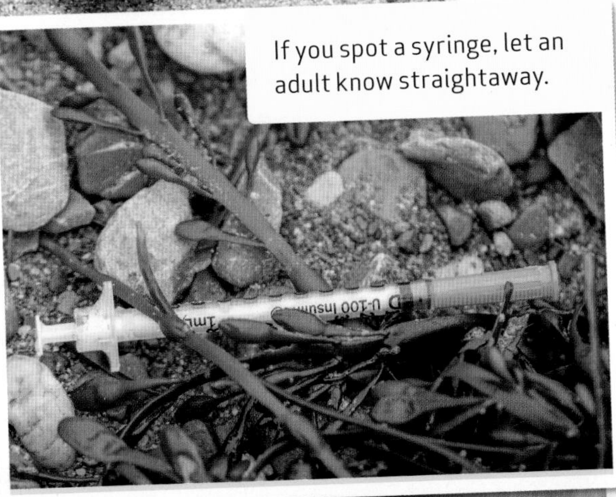

If you spot a syringe, let an adult know straightaway.

Seashore safety

- Don't touch any sharp objects or hazardous substances, and tell an adult where you found them.
- Wash your hands after a beach clean.
- Clean in areas safe from tides, currents, cliffs and other hazards.

Mermaids' tears

Mermaids' tears are small plastic pellets that are found in the ocean. Some come from bigger pieces of plastic litter that are broken down in the sea, while some are **nurdles** – tiny plastic pieces that are melted and used to make plastic bottles and toothbrushes.

Mermaids' tears are small (3mm diameter) beads of plastic.

Polluting pellets

Nurdles sometimes leak out of shipping containers that are damaged or fall overboard while they are being transported across the oceans. The polluting pellets then float, and are eaten by marine creatures.

Huge ships transport the pellets in containers across our oceans.

Searching the sand for nurdles.

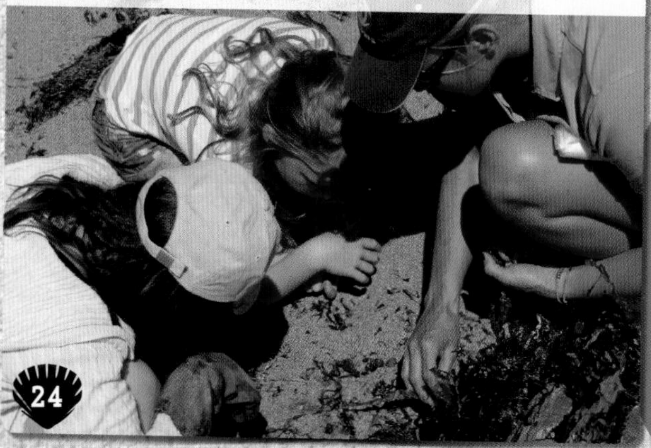

Where do you find mermaids' tears?

Mermaids' tears also wash up on beaches all over the world. They can usually be found among the shells and seaweed on sandy beaches along the highest tide line, left behind by the waves.

Join a nurdle hunt

Tracking down nurdles may be tricky, but it's good for wildlife and great fun. Try searching where larger pieces of plastic may have collected together above the tideline and along the **strandline**.

You will need:

- container such as a jam jar to collect the pellets
- gloves
- sharp eyes
- plenty of patience!

Count the number of nurdles you collect.

Mermaids' tears and wildlife

Mermaids' tears soak up nasty chemicals from surrounding seawater. When birds, fish, turtles, and other sea animals accidentally eat these nurdles, they digest poisons and chemicals.

Seashore safety

- Wear gloves when hunting for nurdles, and wash your hands afterwards.
- Alert an adult to any sharp or hazardous objects.
- Search when the tide is out, and be aware of tides and currents.

Collect mermaids' tears to save wildlife.

The strandline

The strandline is the line of seaweed and debris that is washed ashore by the tides. The debris can include litter, but also rich flora and fauna that lives out at sea.

Seashore buffet

The rotting seaweeds of the strandline become perfect habitats in which flies can lay their eggs. Birds, bats and other small mammals all dine on the flies and their larvae. If the strandline washes back to sea, it becomes a feast for fish, too.

A Eurasian rock pipit searches for its next meal.

A tractor tows a cleaning machine across the strandline.

Did you know?

Mechanical beach-cleaning to clear rotting seaweed and rubbish removes goodness from the seashore. In the clear-up, many insects that larger strandline visitors feed on are all lost.

By-the-wind sailors can be found in all the world's oceans.

By-the-wind sailor

These bright blue creatures float on the ocean's surface and wash ashore in large numbers. They have a 'sail' to catch the wind, on top of a disc, which is filled with air pockets to float and stinging tentacles underneath the disc to catch their prey.

Cuttlefish

This mollusc is best known for its cuttlebone, a hard shell found inside the cuttlefish. Like a submarine, tiny compartments in the cuttlebone fill with, or release, gas to help the cuttlefish float.

Look out for cuttlebones along the strandline.

Sandhoppers

Sandhoppers can be seen hopping wildly along the strandline, and leap their highest under a full moon. Even in a scientist's lab, without being able to see the moon, these shrimp-like creatures will still hop the highest at the full moon phase.

A common sandhopper on the beach strandline.

Ocean art

Why not collect rubbish from the beach and turn it into art to decorate your home, school or community centre? It can become a great talking point, and may inspire others to join you on beach cleans.

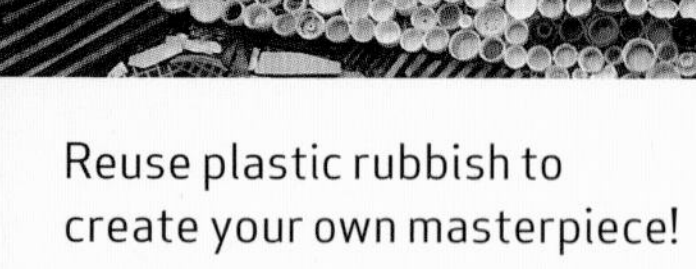

Reuse plastic rubbish to create your own masterpiece!

Talking rubbish

Let trash do the talking – use only machine-made materials that you've found on the beach to create some amazing art! The following bits of kit might be useful:

- scissors
- pliers
- fishing line from beach

Create a fish mobile

Created using old drinks cans, this shoal of floating fish looks great and helps to save wildlife!

You will need:

- scissors
- old fishing line*
- old drink cans*
- hole punch
- driftwood
- large needle
- gloves

*ideally collected at a beach clean

How to make:

- Carefully cut the drinks cans into fish shapes, making the edges as smooth as you can.
- Make the fish eyes using a hole punch, and use a needle to attach the fishing line.
- Hang several fish from a piece of driftwood, at different lengths.

"Art is not what you see, but what you make others see." *Edgar Degas*

Top tips:

- Use washed-up fishing net or line to tie things together.
- Try grouping items together by size, colour or material.
- Get creative and try cutting out other marine creature shapes.

Seashore safety

- Ask an adult to help with any difficult cutting.
- Wear gloves when handling items with sharp edges.

Sand

Sand is smaller than gravel and bigger than silt. It sticks to our toes when we visit the seashore. Grab a handful of sand, and you might see that it's made up of shell, rock, coral and even plastic that has broken down into tiny fragments over time.

An example of sand made up of broken coral and shells.

A sample of coarse sand.

How big is sand?

A sand grain can measure from a microscopic 0.625 mm to a chunkier 2 mm. The types of sand found on beaches are split into grades:

- very fine
- fine
- medium
- coarse
- very coarse

Finer sand is ideal for building sandcastles, as it holds its shape well.

Sand cities

36 billion tonnes of sand are used each year to make concrete, which is used to build roads and cities. This sand must be mined and dredged from our seas and riverbeds.

Surprising sand

A parrotfish uses its parrot-like beak to chomp on the algae attached to coral and rocks. Tiny bits of hard coral pass through the parrotfish's body and come out in a cloud of sandy poo.

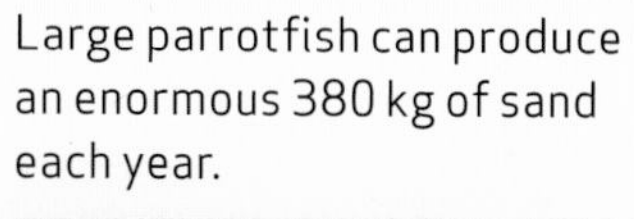

Large parrotfish can produce an enormous 380 kg of sand each year.

This colourful Californian beach glass is made from sand.

Sand and erosion

Coastal **erosion** happens when sand gets washed away by wind, rain and waves. Sand dunes form a barrier to protect land from erosion. Plants that grow there help sand dunes keep their shape, but heavy storms can wash them away.

Plants can act as a windbreak, trapping sand. As more sand is trapped, the dune grows.

Did you know?

Glass is made by heating sand. Sand melts in a furnace when it reaches 1700°C. It then cools into glass, which is an amorphous solid – a cross between a solid and a liquid.

Sand art

As well as being used to make glass and concrete to build our homes, sand is also a great material for creating impressive art projects on the beach. Photograph your creations while you can, as they will only last until the tide turns.

Sand-sculpture tips

Try these tips to help you sculpt something special:

- use fine, shell-free sand, as it's best for sculpting;
- roll wet sand in your hands – if it holds its shape as a ball, it's perfect for sculpting;
- build high on the shore to allow for the tide;
- have a bucket of water on hand, as wet sand is easier to sculpt.

Sand sculptures with lots of detail can take weeks to complete.

Sand-sculpture tools

While your hands and imagination are your best tools, you might also use:

- buckets
- spoons
- spatulas
- brushes
- a spade or shovel
- a water spray bottle
- a used plastic gift card for scraping

Sand sculptures don't need to be complicated to make a big impression.

Rake it in

Rake the sand to form striking geometric patterns, or leave messages for the next seashore watchers to visit. Check the tides and show your creativity.

Sand art is beautiful, though it may not last forever!

Talking points

As you're sculpting, why not think about:

- tides
- erosion
- sand grains

Coarse sand may not be as good for sculpting, but you can still create some special sand art.

Pebbles

Pebble beaches, or shingle beaches, as they are also known, are made up of smooth or angular pebbles of many colours, which are worn down over the years by the action of the waves.

Some pebbles have pretty quartz 'veins'.

How are pebbles formed?

When rocks are washed from the cliffs into the sea, the waves toss them about, until eventually the rocks become smooth and pebble-sized. Pebbles that continue to be eroded will eventually become sand.

Chesil Beach at dusk

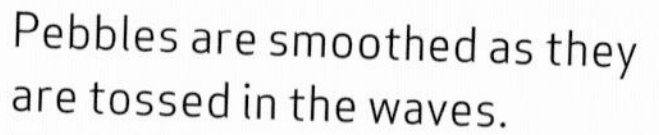

Pebbles are smoothed as they are tossed in the waves.

Did you know?

Chesil Beach in Dorset, UK, is a shingle beach that runs for 29 km. The pebbles there protect the nearby low-lying villages from flooding. The pebbles get smaller in size the further west you head on the beach.

Seashore safety

- Don't build pebble towers too tall – they might fall on you.
- Take photos, then return the pebbles to where you found them.

Pebble art

Test out your balancing skills and see if you can make a tower of pebbles or a stone cairn. People have made stone cairns for centuries, as memorials or trail markers. They can vary from a single stack of pebbles to huge cylindrical pillars.

It takes skilful balance to make a mini pebble cairn.

Protective pebbles

Pebbles help protect the coastline from erosion by absorbing the energy of the constant currents.

Shells

The empty shells of molluscs wash up on our seashores to give us clues about life below the waves. Shells break down to become part of the sand on many golden seashores, and can even become home to hermit crabs.

The dark-shelled, edible mussel is a bivalve.

Bivalve or gastropod?

There are two main classes of mollusc shell, **bivalves** and gastropods. Bivalves have a hinged, two-part shell joined by strong muscles, and include clams, scallops, oysters and mussels. Gastropods have a well-defined head with tentacles, and include limpets, snails and sea slugs.

An abandoned shell makes a fine home for a hermit crab.

Life on a bubble raft

The violet sea snail drifts on the ocean surface in warm seas. It produces a raft of bubbly mucus, which it uses to keep itself afloat.

A drifting violet sea snail.

A diver admires a large trumpet shell off the coast of Papua New Guinea, South Pacific.

Did you know?

The largest living sea snail species is the Australian trumpet shell, whose shell can grow to almost a metre in length. The snail inside can weigh up to 18 kg.

Shellfish predators

Some seashells have holes in them. The holes are made by predators who drill their way through the shell to get at the animal inside.

Deadly shells

Some shells are deadly to the touch. Cone snails are found in tropical waters and have a powerful sting. They hunt for other marine snails and harpoon their victim with a tiny barbed tip, which releases poison. This venom is strong enough to kill humans, too.

The textile cone mollusc is a deadly predator.

Shell art

Shells are best left on the beach for everyone to enjoy, crabs to occupy and to become the sand between our toes. Beautiful shell art can be made on the beach for others to discover, and for the tide to return the shells to the sea.

Collecting seashells

Wander the beach to collect some seashells in your bucket. They will gather in certain areas of the seashore because of the direction of the waves and the swell. Look out for tiny sea snails on the strandline.

Use different sizes and colours to make your shell art.

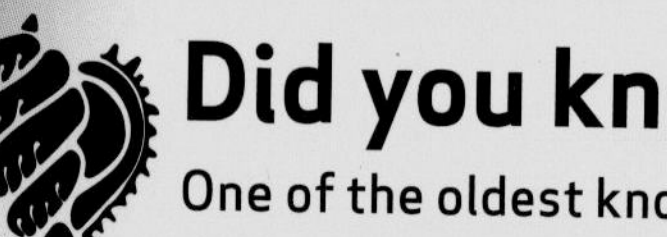

Did you know?

One of the oldest known shell collections was found at Pompeii, Italy. The collection was preserved in the eruption of Mount Vesuvius in 79 CE, and included shells that came from as far as the Red Sea.

How many different types of shell will you find?

Sailor's valentine

In the nineteenth century, sailors of the South Seas would bring back shell art as gifts for their loved ones. The **sailor's valentine** was an intricate pattern of shells, which were often presented in an octagonal, glass-fronted box. The artwork would often include hearts, anchors or even a sentimental message made from pretty shells.

A Victorian sailor's valentine.

Make a seashore sailor's valentine

Once you've collected enough shells, group them by colour, shape or size. Find a flat area of sandy beach on the high tide and make a pattern with your shells. Take a photo as a keepsake of your artwork, and then leave it there for others to enjoy.

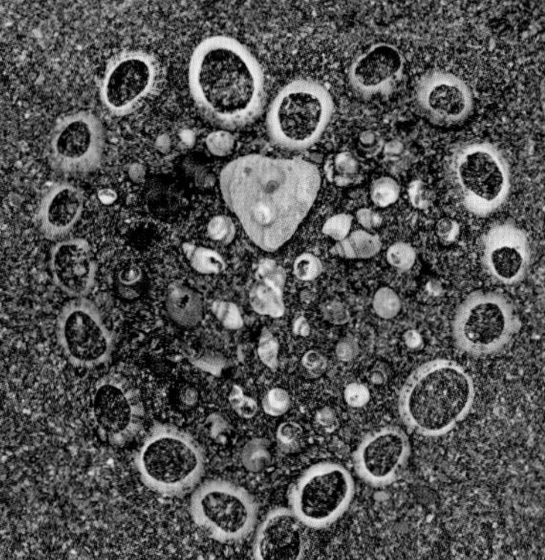

A simple piece of seashore art.

Almost every seashell for sale comes from a living animal that was killed to sell as a souvenir.

She sells seashells ...

Seaside shops sometimes sell dried starfish and empty shells, like the Australian trumpet as souvenirs. Shells are often collected and overfished, putting some species at risk. It's best to avoid these shops, and take photographs of your finds on the seashore.

Plankton

Plankton are (mostly) tiny organisms that drift in the sea, but huge jellyfish are classed as plankton, too. In this mix of tiny creatures, you will find the larvae of crabs, starfish and barnacles, as well as other creatures that drift in ocean currents and around our shores.

Phytoplankton may be small, but their role in the world is huge.

Where are plankton found?

Plankton can be found all over the world, but plankton-rich water is found where there are lots of nutrients in shallow seas or upwellings – where deep water rises up to meet shallow.

The zoea larval stage of the crab.

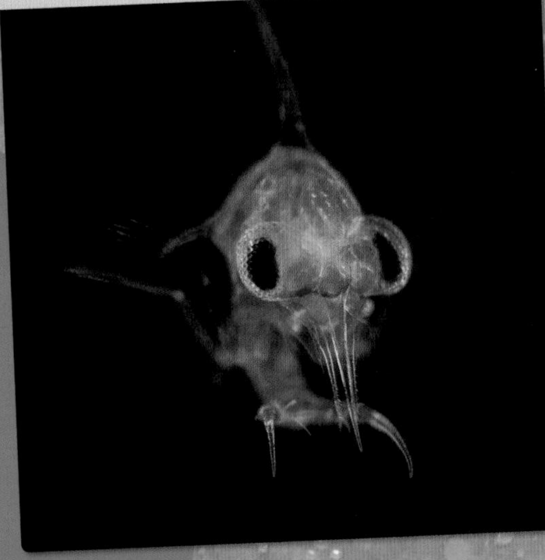

Crab plankton

Crab plankton appear very alien in their zoea larval stage – they look like a tiny lobster with a spiky horn. As crabs moult, they become more like the crabs we know, with five pairs of legs and tiny claws.

Larva of a brittle star.

Brittle star plankton

The first form of brittle star plankton looks like a splat of paint. As this delicate starfish develops, we can see the spiky arms that we recognise in fully grown starfish.

Larva of an anemone.

Anemone plankton

The anemones that we find in rock pools begin life drifting as plankton. They look just like their close relatives, the jellyfish, when they're this young and small.

Did you know?

Phytoplankton are microscopic marine plants that need sunlight to live and grow in the ocean. Phytoplankton absorb carbon dioxide, and supply about two-thirds of the oxygen we need to breathe.

Make a plankton net

Hunting for plankton is great fun. You can buy a professional plankton net, or make one at home fairly simply and cheaply.

A home-made plankton net – patterned duct tape is optional!

You will need:

- thick wire
- duct tape
- a stocking, or 1 leg from a pair of tights with the foot removed
- a large plastic bottle, chopped in half
- string
- thick cord
- 4 metal key rings
- scissors
- a needle and thread

Equipment for making a plankton net.

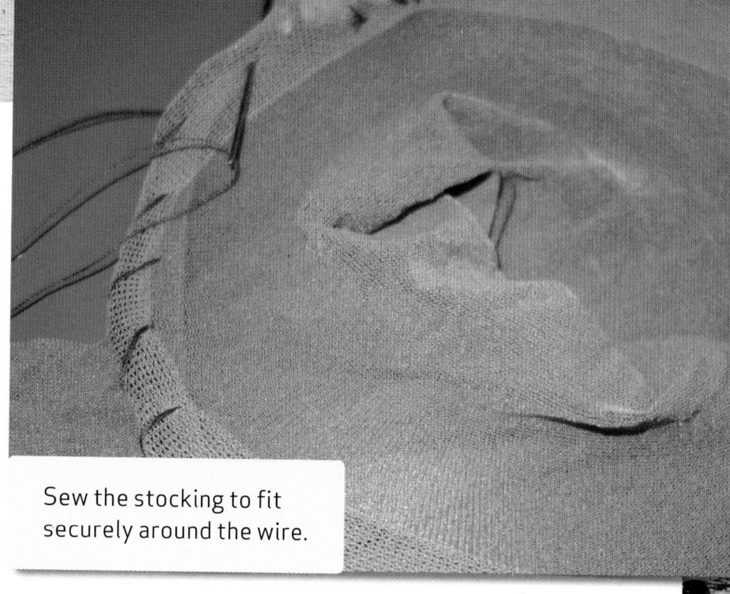

Sew the stocking to fit securely around the wire.

How to make:

1. Use the wire to make a ring shape, about 10 cm in diameter.
2. Use duct tape to cover the wire's loose ends.
3. Sew the stocking around the wire at the widest end with a needle and thread.
4. Carefully cut the bottle in half, in the middle. Push the bottom half of the bottle down to the foot end of the stocking and secure with tape.
5. Sew three key rings at equal distances around the hoop, then thread a 50-cm length of string through each key ring and tie a secure knot.
6. Gather the three ends of string together and attach to a central key ring.
7. Tie some thick cord to the central key ring.
8. Now you're ready to test out your net!

Using your plankton net

- Drop your net over a sea wall, standing well clear of the wall and making sure your rope is long enough to reach the water below.
- Walk your net backwards and forwards along the sea wall.
- Draw in your net and empty the bottle into a tray or jar to look at your plankton – use a magnifying glass or microscope if you have one.

Plankton fishing is great fun!

Seashore safety

- Get an adult to help you cut the bottle and any wire.
- Always stay close to an adult when plankton fishing.
- Return the plankton to the sea once you've taken a good look.

Seaweed

Seaweeds vary from small and delicate leaves to huge kelps found below the low tide. Marine algae create underwater forests and act as a safe place for fish and other creatures to breed and live.

Types of seaweed

Seaweeds use pigments to **photosynthesize**, just like plants. **Photosynthesis** is the process that plants use to convert the energy in sunlight into food that they use for energy. There are three main types of seaweed, which have different pigments that give them their colour. Can you pronounce and remember their names?

Brown seaweeds: fucoxanthin (say: few-coh-zan-thin)

Green seaweeds: chlorophyll (say: chlo-roh-fill)

Red seaweeds: phycoerythrin (say: fy-coh-eh-rith-rin) and phycocyanin (say: fy-coh-sy-ah-nin)

Sea beech grows in the intertidal zone on rocky shores.

Sea beech

This seaweed has veined 'blades' that look just like beech-tree leaves. It is a deep pink and has inspired poets to write about it. It can be found in the Northern hemisphere in Europe and on Icelandic shores.

Seaweed anatomy

- The **holdfast** of the seaweed looks like a root. It attaches or 'holds fast' to the rocks.
- The **stipe** is like the stalk or stem of the seaweed. Its job is to support the rest of the plant.
- The **frond** (or blade)of the seaweed is the leafy part. It can be veined and thin, leathery or branched.

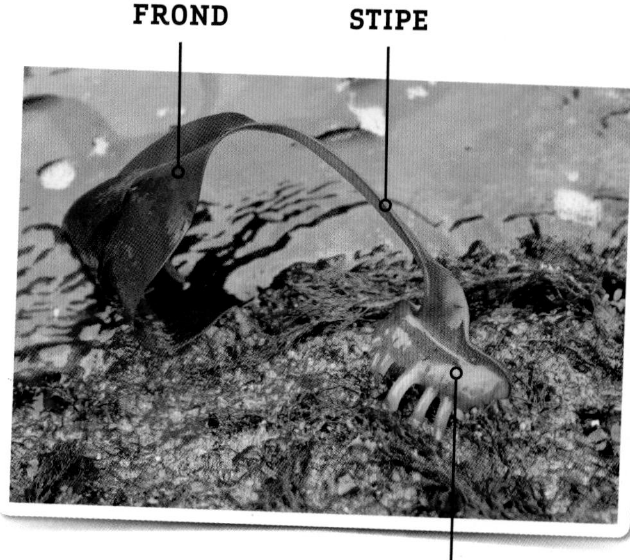

Giant kelp can grow up to 50 metres tall.

Giant kelp

This a brown seaweed that is commonly found around the Pacific coast of North America and in the southern oceans of South America, South Africa and Australia.

Sea Lettuce

Found on rocky shores worldwide, sea lettuce is a thin, translucent, green seaweed that resembles lettuce leaves.

Make a seaweed press

Seaweed presses can make great pictures, illustrating the colours and intricate shapes of seaweeds. Scientists use seaweed presses to record where seaweeds have been found, while pressing seaweeds was a favourite hobby of the Victorians.

A delicate pressed seaweed.

Pressing seaweeds at the seashore.

Pressed seaweeds from Victorian times are often displayed in museums.

You will need:

- thin seaweeds, collected from the seashore
- a deep tray to hold 3 cm of water
- card or thick paper
- a fine paintbrush
- blue household cloths or muslin
- old newspapers
- 3 books (as weights)

How to make:

1. Collect a fine, thin seaweed specimen that has washed ashore.
2. Fill your tray with clear seawater or tap water until it's 2.5cm deep.
3. Place the card in the tray of water.
4. Place the seaweed on the card and use the paintbrush to flatten out the seaweed and show all its detail.
5. Lift the card out of the water. Try to keep the seaweed as still as possible on the card.
6. Place a cloth or muslin over the card, then place a newspaper on top and underneath.
7. Place a few heavy books on top of the press and transfer it to a warm cupboard.
8. Change the newspaper daily until the press is bone dry.
9. Carefully peel back the cloth to reveal your seaweed press.

What next?

Make a label for your seaweed. It should include:

- the species of seaweed;
- where you found the seaweed – on the shore, in a rock pool etc.;
- the name of the beach;
- your name;
- the date it was collected.

Seashore safety

- Remember to wash your hands after handling seaweed.

Seaweed jelly

Some seaweeds have a gelatin-like substance that can be used to make jelly. Seaweed's gelling properties are used for making medicines and food.

Collecting seaweed

- Cut just enough seaweed from the top third of the plant, so that it can regrow.
- Do not rip seaweed from rocks.
- Seaweed can be dried until you are ready to use it.
- Rinse seaweed well in fresh water, and wash your hands afterwards.

Irish Moss can be used for making jelly.

You will need:

- ½ cup of seaweed that contains carrageenan or agar, like Irish Moss
- Juice of ½ an orange
- 1 tbsp honey

Seaweed jelly is simple to make and surprisingly tasty.

How to make:

1. Rinse the seaweed to remove all traces of salt.
2. Chop the seaweed into small 3-cm pieces and ask an adult to place them into a saucepan of boiling water.
3. Simmer for 20 minutes until the liquid has thickened well.
4. Drain the liquid from the pan, and throw away the seaweed.
5. Squeeze half an orange, and add the juice to the liquid.
6. Add a little honey to sweeten, and stir well.
7. Pour the liquid into a jelly mould, and chill in the fridge for at least an hour.
8. Eat and enjoy!

The finished orange jelly has no seaweed flavour.

Super seaweed

Carrageenan has been used as a food additive for over 600 years, and agar for more than 300 years. Today, it is used for thickening, and as a stabilizing agent in foods such as ice cream and milk-based puddings, some pet foods, toothpastes, air-freshener gels, medicines and cosmetics.

Agar jelly is used in medicine to grow bacteria.

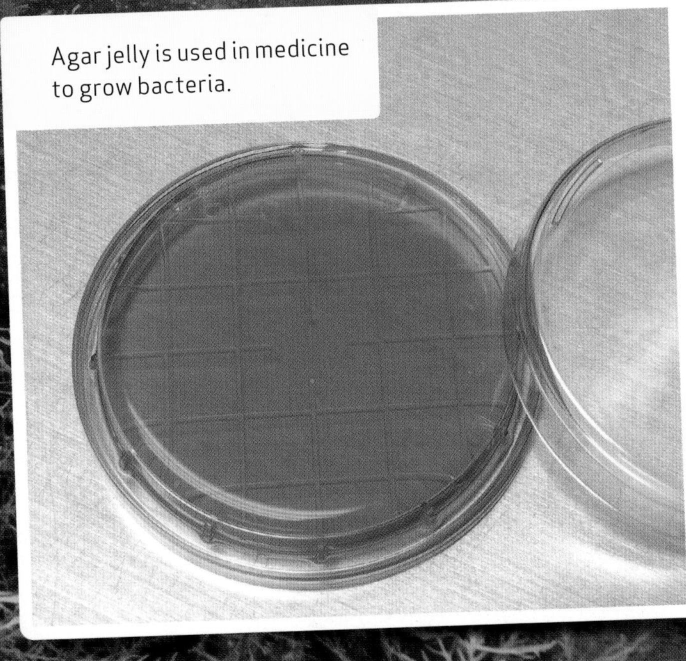

Seashore safety

- Only collect seaweed from seashores that are free from pollution.
- Never collect seaweed after 'red tide' or pollution incidents.
- Respect wildlife, and don't pick more seaweed than you need.
- Be sure of the species you are collecting.
- Ask an adult to pour any boiling water for you.

Sea anemones

Colourful sea anemones decorate tidal pools on the seashore like beautiful flowers, though they live in deeper waters, too. They are sometimes called the 'flowers of the sea' but they are in fact animals. Like jellyfish, their tentacles have a mild sting.

How anemones feed

Anemones have a ring of tentacles surrounding their central mouth. When a creature passes over the anemone's tentacles, the tentacles will sting the animal and stun them. The anemone will then draw its prey into its mouth and into its stomach. The mouth will then 'spit out' any inedible bits, such as bones or shells.

An anemone can even devour crabs' legs.

Beadlet anemones can have up to 192 tentacles.

Beadlet anemones

The Beadlet anemone will, at low tide, withdraw its tentacles to prevent itself from drying out. You will then see only a red or green 'blob' of jelly, stuck to the rock. This anemone can be found throughout Western Europe and the Mediterranean Sea, as well as along the Atlantic coast of Africa.

Dahlia anemones are often found on rocks, sometimes partially buried in sand.

Dahlia anemone

This anemone has fleshy tentacles. When the tentacles are drawn in, fragments of shell and sand attach to the anemone's wart-covered column. They can be found in the North Atlantic Ocean and the North and Baltic Seas.

Club-tipped anemone

This anemone has short tentacles with small spheres at the end. Club-tipped anemones often provide shrimp with a home and can be found in the North Atlantic Azores Islands and the Mediterranean Sea.

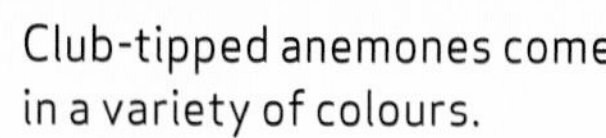

Club-tipped anemones come in a variety of colours.

Seashore safety

- While most sea anemones are fairly harmless to humans, a few contain strong toxic substances. Never touch sea anemones with bare hands.

Night rockpooling

If you are fascinated by tidal pools in daylight, the same pools by night are even more incredible. Many species of fish, crustacean and mollusc are at their most active after dark.

Rockpools at night offer an incredible spectacle.

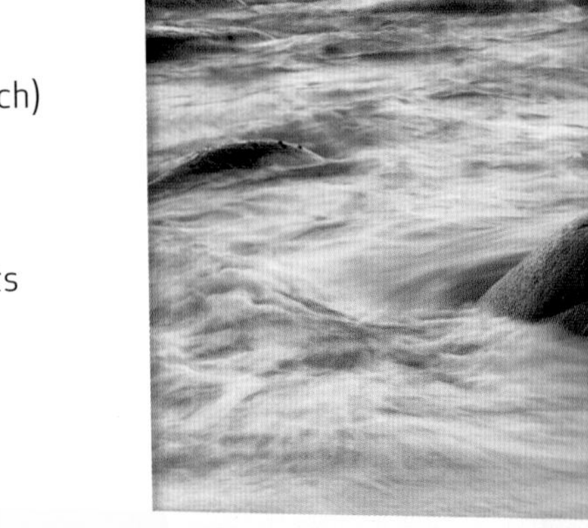

Night-rockpooling kit

- head torch to go hands-free (and a spare pocket torch)
- UV torch
- spare batteries
- warm and waterproof layers of clothing with pockets
- reflective gear
- emergency phone in a sealed, dry bag

Before you go:

Make sure you confidently know:

- the Seashore Code (look back at pages 12–13);
- the local tides and currents (look back at pages 14–15);
- the weather forecast (look back at pages 16–17);
- your chosen beach.

Crab hairs glow under ultraviolet light.

Top Tips:

With limited light, take extra care. Remember:

- pools of water can be deeper than they appear;
- your balance may not be at its best;
- use markers on land to get your bearings;
- only go in fair weather, with cloudless nights;
- store kit in your pockets keeping your hands free to safely navigate rocks.

An inexpensive UV torch will help you to get the most out of your moonlit trip.

A shrimp glows bright green in the waters of the Adriatic Sea.

Fluorescence

Rockpools create an extraordinary light show – experiment with your ultraviolet torch to see what **fluoresces** or glows. Look out for glowing anemones, rotting seaweed that fluoresces bright orange and even green shrimp!

Seashore safety

- Try going night rockpooling with experienced seashore watchers who can guide you.
- Never go night rockpooling without an adult.

Corals

Corals are tiny animals related to anemones and jellyfish. They live in tropical and cooler seas, along shallow shorelines and even in the deeper oceans. Tropical coral reefs are colourful underwater worlds that are packed with a variety of species.

Synchronised spawning

Every year in the coral reefs mass coral spawning occurs. The sea fills with sperm and eggs released by the corals all at the same time. This natural wonder happens after a full moon, once a year, and looks like an underwater snowstorm. It usually lasts for about a week.

Spectacular mass coral spawning on the Great Barrier Reef.

A stony-looking hard coral.

Coral anatomy

Corals are made up of tiny polyps, which look like anemones. The polyps of hard corals make a stony, protective shell out of calcium carbonate. These polyps create coral reefs. Many corals have an algae living within them called **zooxanthellae**, which creates energy by converting sunlight into energy for food (photosynthesis).

Devonshire cup coral

The Devonshire cup coral is a solitary coral that can be found around the shores of the UK, southwest Europe and the Mediterranean. The polyp looks like a small anemone, but has an internal skeleton shaped like a cup, into which it can shrink and hide.

The Devonshire cup coral varies in colour from white, pink, orange, red to green.

Dead man's fingers

Dead man's fingers is a soft and fleshy coral that grows in colonies throughout Europe, and also in American and Canadian waters. Its finger-like polyps grow under piers or rocky overhangs in shallow waters.

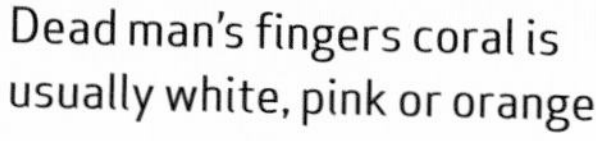

Dead man's fingers coral is usually white, pink or orange.

Staghorn coral

Staghorn coral, as the name suggests, looks just like a stag's antlers. Its 'branches' offer fish a place to find safety. This fast-growing coral is found on many tropical coral reefs.

Staghorn coral is an endangered species.

Exploring corals

Coral reefs are under threat. Since they grow at such a slow rate, they are being destroyed faster than they can repair themselves. Much of the damage is caused by humans – from climate change, pollution, overfishing and tourism.

Coral colonies can take hundreds of years to form.

Coral code

We can follow these simple steps to help protect coral reefs:

- never touch or step on corals;
- collect memories and photos instead of taking corals – whether living or dead;
- keep clear of turtles and other marine animals;
- if snorkelling, keep fins and flippers clear to avoid damaging coral;
- never feed any fish or marine life.

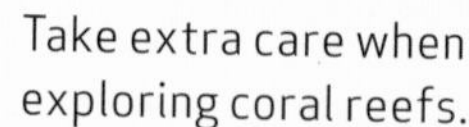
Take extra care when exploring coral reefs.

Did you know?

Coral reefs cover just 0.2% of all our oceans, but contain 25% of all of the world's marine fish species.

Corals and parts of the reef that have died turn into reef rubble.

Coral bleaching

If the seawater becomes too warm, corals release the zooxanthellae algae that it needs to live. The coral then turns white, can die or lose its structure, and fish lose their homes.

The Great Barrier Reef

The Great Barrier Reef is the planet's largest natural structure and coral reef. It stretches along the east coast of Australia for over 2300 km. The reef is home to 600 types of corals, 133 shark and ray species and 1625 fish species.

What we can do to help

By reducing the amount of carbon we produce, we can help prevent the warming of our oceans and coral bleaching. You could try to:

- walk or cycle instead of travel by car;
- turn off lights, TVs and computers when you do not need them;
- take fewer journeys by aeroplane;
- turn down the heating – put on a jumper if you need to;
- eat local produce and choose food with less packaging.

Jellyfish

Jellyfish are jelly-like creatures that are mostly made up of water and protein. Jellyfish are weak swimmers, drifting in the oceans, and so they are also classed as plankton.

Jellyfish anatomy

Jellyfish arms are often mistaken for the stinging tentacles of jellyfish. The tentacles of jellyfish are usually found around the edge of the bell.

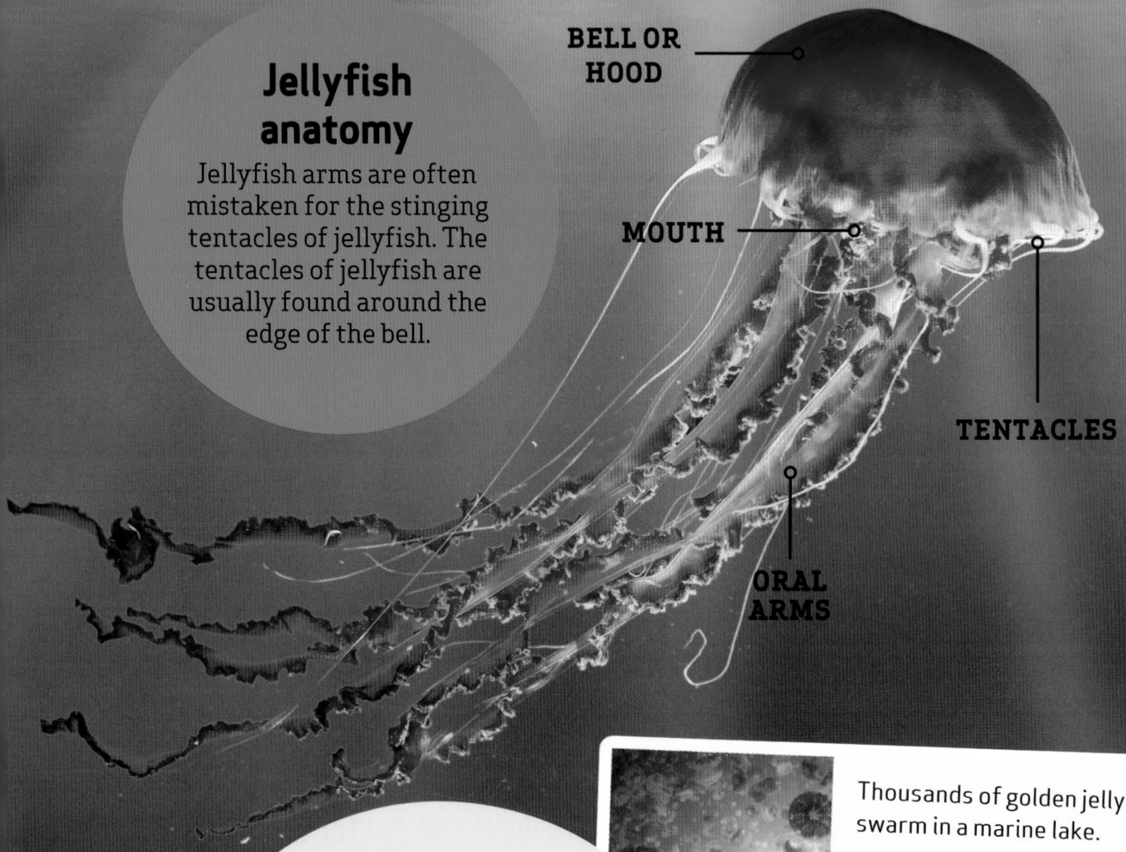

BELL OR HOOD

MOUTH

TENTACLES

ORAL ARMS

Thousands of golden jellyfish swarm in a marine lake.

Jellyfish blooms

When jellyfish wash onto the shore or appear in shallow seas in huge numbers, it is called a **bloom**. Jellyfish have always gathered because they drift with currents, but warmer oceans, overfishing and an increase in nutrients in the sea mean that jellyfish blooms are becoming more common.

Lion's mane jellyfish

This huge, stinging jellyfish grows to over 2 metres across the bell, and has tentacles that can trail for over 30 metres. It is most commonly found in the cooler waters of the Arctic, Atlantic and Pacific Oceans. Its sting is painful, but not thought to be deadly to humans.

The lion's mane jellyfish has up to 1200 tentacles.

White-spotted jellyfish

This beautiful domed, semi-transparent jellyfish has small white spots that are evenly spaced all over its bell. It can be found in Australia and the Pacific Islands and has a very mild sting.

The box jellyfish has a nasty sting.

Box jellyfish or sea wasp

The box jellyfish or sea wasp is well known due to its extremely potent venom that can be deadly to humans. The bell of this jellyfish is cube or box-shaped, with four tentacles that trail for up to 3 metres from its corners.

Jellyfish stings

Jellyfish, anemones and corals belong to a group of animals called **cnidaria** (say: ny-dair-ee-ah). Their tentacles are covered with thousands of deadly stinging cells. When another creature touches the jellyfish, harpoon-like darts shoot out at high speed into the creature's skin and a toxic venom is released.

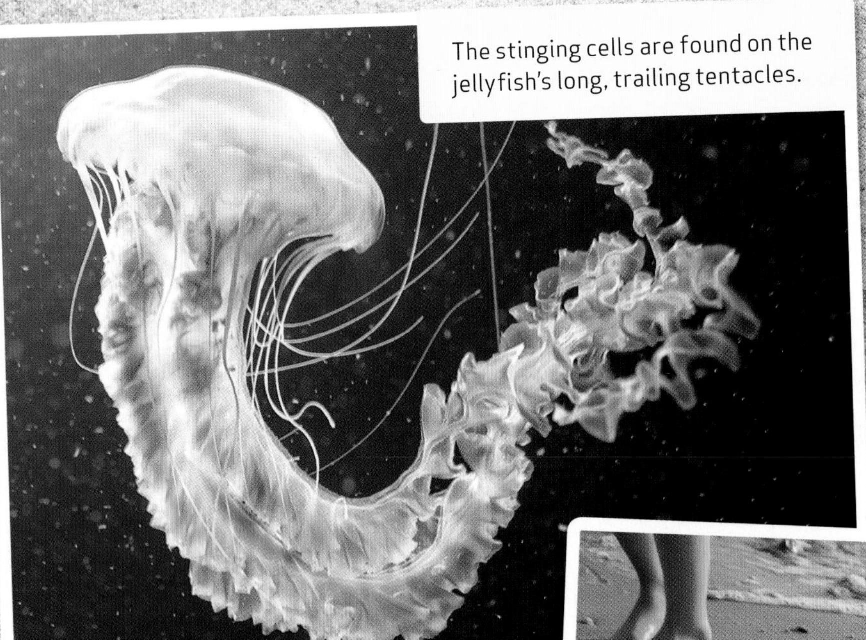

The stinging cells are found on the jellyfish's long, trailing tentacles.

Seashore safety

- Wearing a wetsuit when swimming or diving can help you avoid being stung.
- Stay out of the water during jellyfish season, when jellyfish numbers are high.

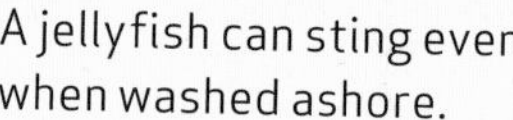

A jellyfish can sting even when washed ashore.

How to treat a jellyfish sting

If you are stung by a jellyfish:

- ask an adult for help straightaway;
- try to leave the water without splashing to prevent more stingers from releasing venom;
- remove the stings with a stick or credit card – wearing gloves if possible;
- wash the area with seawater (not fresh water);
- a heat pack or immersion in hot water will help reduce the pain;
- applying vinegar is thought to stop further stings from box jellyfish, though wee or alcohol could make the pain worse.

This beach sign warns of poisonous jellyfish sightings.

Turtle-y delicious

Some turtle species, such as Leatherbacks, love to eat jellyfish despite their stings. Sea turtles have really thick skin and bite the jellyfish from above the bell to avoid being stung. While adult green sea turtles are herbivores, feeding mostly on algae and seaweed, younger turtles eat a variety of animals and plants, including jellyfish.

A green sea turtle enjoying a jellyfish feast.

Marine worms

Worms that live in the sea are called marine worms. They come in all shapes and sizes and include both beautiful and wondrous species. There are colourful, segmented worms, flat worms and even peanut worms that look like an elephant's trunk.

A peanut worm in shallow waters.

The lengthy bootlace worm

Bootlace worm

The bootlace worm is thought to be one of the longest creatures on the planet, with the longest reported worm found on Scottish shores, measuring a huge 55 metres – that's longer than the blue whale! While they may be long, they only measure about 2 cm wide.

Bearded fireworm

This colourful, furry-looking worm looks a lot like a caterpillar or a centipede. It is called 'fireworm' because of the burning sensation that the venom in its bristles can cause. Found in tropical Atlantic waters and the Mediterranean, the bearded fireworm is a hungry predator of corals and small crustaceans.

The predatory bearded fireworm.

Colourful Christmas tree worms.

Christmas tree worm

These bright worms live on coral reefs around the world. They do not move, but instead attach themselves to coral. Each worm has two tree-like attachments that are used to breathe and filter food as it floats by.

Bispira worm

This worm has twin fans of bright white bristles that appear from a flattened tube. It can be found in tidal pools on very low tides around the southwest of England and on some European shores.

The spiralling bispira worm.

Seashore snorkelling

Snorkelling is an excellent way to explore the seashore. Having just a few simple pieces of kit will allow you to see some unforgettable underwater sights.

Snorkelling kit

Here's what you'll need to get started:

- a well-fitting mask
- a snorkel
- flippers (optional)
- a wetsuit (in cooler seas) or swimsuit

Snorkelling tips

- practise using your snorkel in a safe environment: a pool, the bath or in shallow seas;
- clear your snorkel by tilting your head back and breathing out with a forceful breath;
- breathe slowly and try to stay relaxed.

Duck dive

As you become more confident, you might like to try diving a little deeper. Here's how to master the duck dive:

- Swim forwards at speed to gain momentum.
- Next, point your arms downwards in the direction you wish to dive.
- Bend at the hips, while keeping your legs straight. This will bring your upper body in line with your arms.
- Lift your legs together vertically, then pull downwards with your arms.

A snorkeller exploring deeper waters.

Seashore safety

- Never snorkel alone.
- Only snorkel if you're a strong swimmer.
- Snorkel at beaches where lifeguards patrol.
- Protect your skin from the sun's rays.
- Know your beach – currents, tides and any dangers.
- Check the weather conditions before you go.
- Snorkel on days of flat, calm water.
- Look after your kit – rinse in fresh water after use.

Have you ever wanted to meet a sea turtle?

Limpets

Limpets may not be the most attractive molluscs, but they are certainly tough. Their cone-shaped shells can be spotted on the seashore clamped firmly to rocks, as the tides roll in and out.

Limpets shells are almost impossible to dislodge.

Common limpet

The common limpet has a yellowish foot, and can be found on rocky shores between the high and low tides. This limpet is common to the shores of Europe.

A common limpet leaves a trail of slime.

A home scar is left by a limpet.

Home scars

Limpets stick tightly to rocks so that they don't dry out. So tightly, in fact, that they create a groove in the rock that perfectly fits their shell. This is called the home scar.

Limpet anatomy

The underside of a limpet:

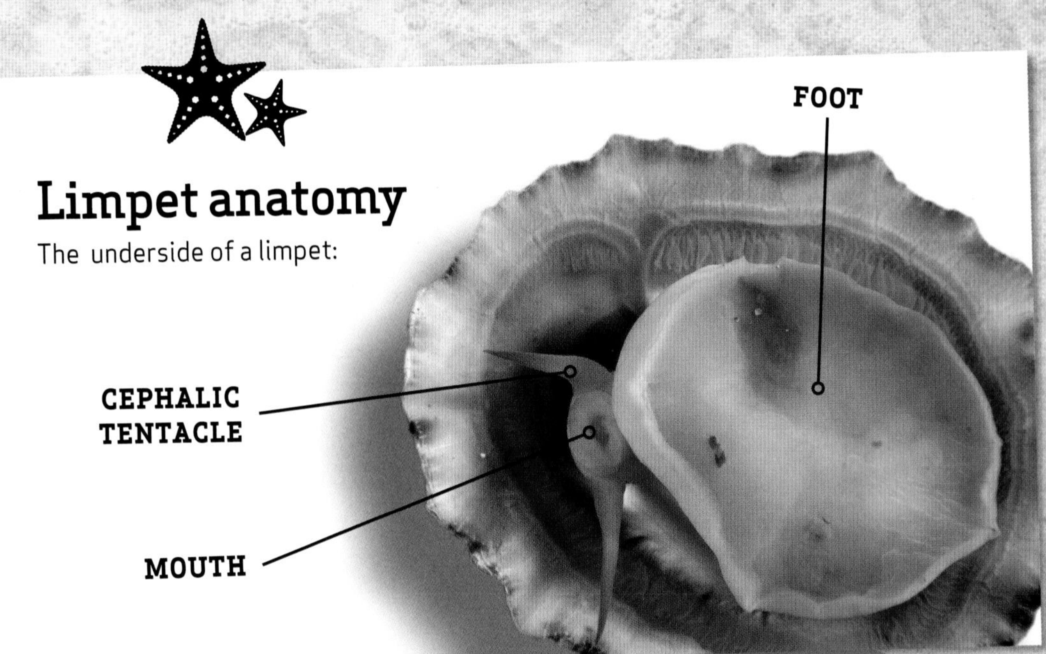

A stack of slipper limpets.

Slipper limpet

The slipper limpet, also known as the Atlantic slippersnail, is native to the east coast of North America, but has also been introduced accidentally to some areas of Europe. They can be found in a stack, with the larger female limpet at the base and the smaller males on top.

A variegated limpet, Manly, Australia.

Variegated limpet

This limpet has a ribbed shell, though these 'ribs' may be hidden by algae. It can be found off the south and east coasts of Australia and Tasmania from the high tide to mid-tide levels.

How do limpets feed?

Limpets move away from their home scar and feed on algae during high tide. Constant grazing stops bigger seaweeds from growing on the rocks, which is why limpets are sometimes called the 'sheep of the seashore'.

A limpet on the move.

These limpets don't have to move too far for their next meal.

Limpet locomotion

As the tide rises, the limpet lifts its shell from the home scar and slithers over the rocks. Mucus and a muscular foot helps the limpet stay attached to the surface, keeping it safe from predators like starfish.

Tough tongue

Limpets have a small mouth underneath their shell that contains a tongue-like radula. The radula is covered in teeth that scrape the algae from the rocks. It's possible to hear limpets scraping seaweed from the rocks by using an underwater microphone.

Did you know?

Limpets' teeth are made up of the strongest biological material known to humans. This material is helping scientists to develop unbreakable false teeth.

The radula of a common limpet is bristled with tiny teeth.

Finding their way home

Limpets leave a slimy trail when they feed, which not only helps them find their way home, but also allows algae to regrow.

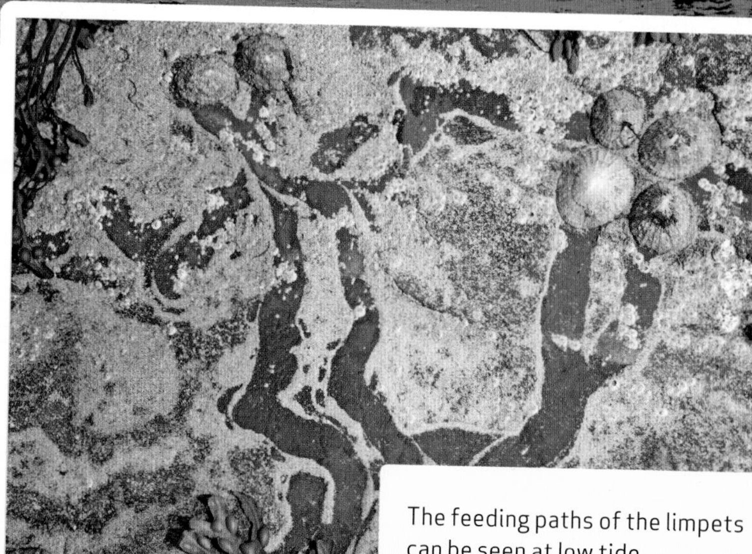

The feeding paths of the limpets can be seen at low tide.

Scallops

Have you ever seen or eaten a scallop? Scallop shells are popular with beachcombers, while the meat inside is served in restaurants all over the world. Scallops can be found in all five of our oceans.

Did you know?

The edible white scallop meat is actually a muscle. It holds the upper and lower shell together. The orange 'coral' or roe meat is the ovary, where the eggs are found.

Scallop anatomy

The underside of a scallop.

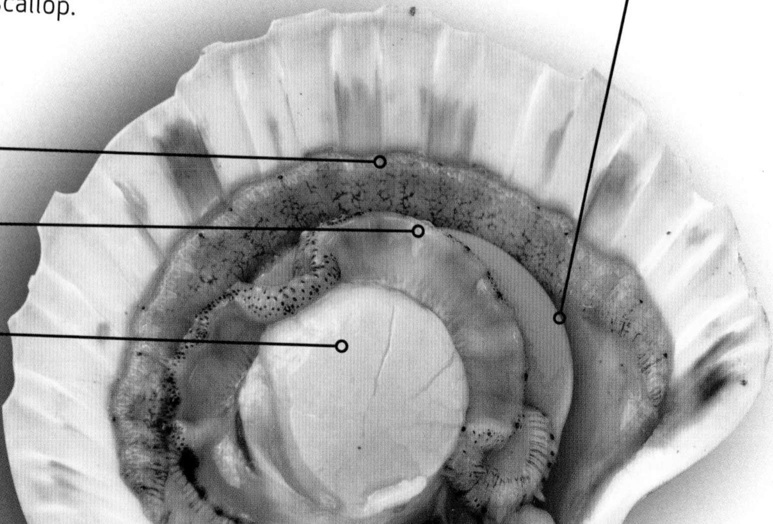

OUTER MANTLE

GILLS

ADDUCTOR MUSCLE

OVARY

Scallops are known for their fan-shaped shells.

Scallops as seafood

Scallops are gathered for seafood in great numbers by scallop dredgers that are dragged along the seabed. Fishing in this way can cause a dangerous decline in scallop numbers. Eating diver-caught scallops is better for the marine environment and the scallop population.

Scallop dredging nets, by a trawler.

Giant scallop

Giant scallops have deep ribs that fan out from the hinge. They can grow up to 21 cm wide, and can be found in the deeper waters of the Atlantic European coast and at very low tides on the shores of **estuaries**.

The barnacle-covered shell of an Atlantic deep-sea scallop.

The giant scallop has clear ribs on its shell.

Atlantic deep-sea scallop

This scallop is found in the northwest Atlantic. At about 17 cm, it is smaller than the giant scallop. It generally lives in deeper water but can also be found on shallower Canadian seashores and on the Maine coast in New England, US. It has a smooth shell without any ridges.

Scallop skills

Scallops are special and surprising sea creatures. You may not guess by looking at one, but scallops can see as well as swim!

A free-swimming giant rock scallop.

Scallop sight

Scallops have up to 60 eyes lining the edge of their shells. If you look closely, you will see lots of tiny blue or dark, metallic-looking spheres. These are, in fact, the scallop's eyes.

The bright blue eyes of a queen scallop.

Did you know?

Some scallops can live for 20 years or more. You can estimate the age of the scallop by the number of rings on its shell.

What do they see?

Scallops' vision isn't as sharp as our own. Their eyes are like little mirrors that detect light, dark and motion. Scallops filter the water for microscopic pieces of food that they see around them. They can also see predators, and will swim away from danger.

Scallops can see in dim underwater conditions.

A queen scallop swimming by jet propulsion.

Surprising swimmers

Unlike other bivalves, most scallops can swim and they are surprisingly quick! A scallop claps the two parts of its shell together quickly, which moves a jet of water past the shell hinge. This comes in handy when scallops are disturbed by predators, such as starfish.

Barnacles

Barnacles are related to crabs and lobsters. You will usually spot them attached to rocks, where they filter food from the water. Stalked barnacles attach to drifting flotsam, as well as rocks.

Stalked barnacles attached to rocks.

Barnacle anatomy

On the seashore, you will see barnacles covering the rocks with their curled legs or '**cirri**', hidden behind closed, stony plates. Underwater, the curled feet emerge to feed, taking plankton from the water.

Did you know?

Barnacles commonly grow on boats, piers and even on whales.

Barnacles growing on a grey whale in Mexico.

Acorn barnacles

This barnacle can be found on the northeast Atlantic and the Pacific coasts of North America. The external shell of the barnacle is made up of six plates.

A colony of acorn barnacles.

A giant acorn barnacle opens to feed on plankton.

Giant acorn barnacle

This barnacle is, as its name suggests, a relative giant. It can be as tall as 30 cm and measure 15 cm in diameter. It is found on the seashore, and in deeper waters, along the shorelines of Alaska to as far south as Mexico.

Bringing barnacles to life

It takes about six months for barnacle larvae to develop into hard-shelled adults.

The barnacle life cycle

Barnacles begin life as tiny eggs, released from their parents' shells. They feed hungrily on plankton, growing and moulting into shrimp-like larvae. These larvae settle, and begin feeling around for a new home, beginning the cycle all over again.

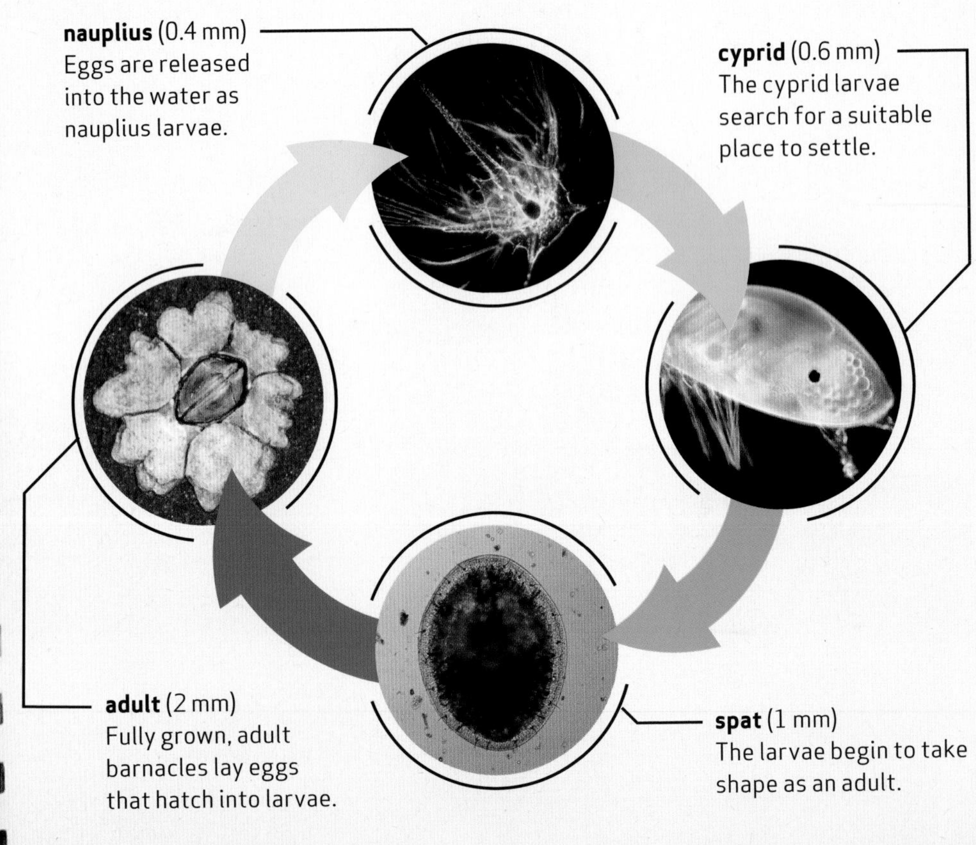

The nauplius

Once the eggs have been fertilized, up to 10,000 naupli are hatched within the shell of the barnacle. When they are ready, they are released into the water as plankton. The plankton feeds on algae and begins to grow.

The cyprid

After a week of feeding and growing, the nauplius outgrows its shell, and grows a new one underneath. It **moults** the old shell, and develops into a cyprid. The cyprid is no longer in the feeding stage – its role is to search for a place to settle.

The adult

Fully grown, adult barnacles lay eggs that hatch into larvae. The barnacle evolves again, forming thick plates around its body to look like a tiny volcano. Plates at the top of the shell open in water, as the barnacle kicks out its curled feet to collect food – tiny plankton. When the adult lays eggs, the life cycle begins again.

The spat

The spat prepares to cement itself to the rock alongside adult barnacles. Its body is flat and its mouth disappears, replaced by a cement-like sac. The spat kicks its legs and swims to find a rock to call home, where it will remain stuck for the rest of its life.

The adult barnacle almost does a headstand, kicking its legs in the air.

Barnacles at low tide, cemented to a beach structure.

Crabs

Crabs are found on every continent in the world. They live on the seashore, in the deep oceans, in freshwater and even on land. Crabs have ten legs in total with crushing and pinching claws on the end of their two front legs.

A crab removes its old shell to reveal its soft side underneath.

Moulting magic

A crab moults its entire shell, just as a snake sheds its skin. A crab's soft body emerges out of its hard shell, leaving what looks like an entire dead crab behind. Crabs are very soft when freshly emerged and swell with water before their skin hardens to form a new, bigger shell. Amazingly, crabs can even re-grow lost legs when they moult.

Edible crab

The edible crab, or brown crab, has a pie-crust edge around the front of its rust-coloured body. It is easy to handle and will tightly curl up its legs and claws below its body. It is often found in the North Sea, North Atlantic Ocean and sometimes in the Mediterranean Sea.

Brown crabs on the British seashore.

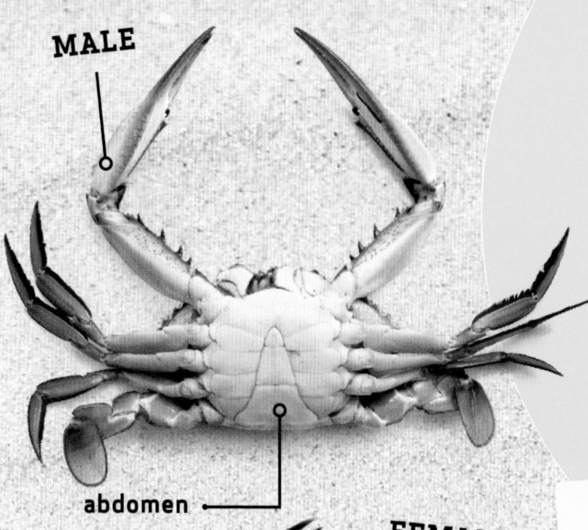

Male or female?

To tell the difference between a male and female crab, gently turn it over. The male crab has a pointy 'abdomen' made up of five segments, while the female has a rounded abdomen made up of seven segments. Sometimes you will see an orange mass on the underside of a female crab. This is an egg mass, which contains thousands of eggs.

FEMALE

abdomen

Crab larvae drift for several weeks before settling on the sea bed to hatch.

Shore crab

Crabbers in Europe should look out for the shore crab – it's a very common species there. It has a green mottled shell and five teeth either side of its eyes on its carapace. The shore crab has also travelled the Atlantic Ocean and can now be found on American shores.

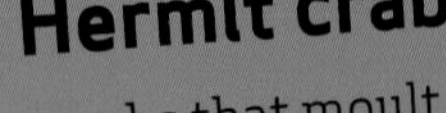

Hermit crab

Some crabs that moult their own shells hunt for new homes in the shells of other creatures. Hermit crabs will knock on the shell of a bigger hermit crab to scare it into leaving home. Once the shell has been vacated it's time to claim their new house.

Seashore safety

- When picking up a crab, hold your finger and thumb out like a pincer. Pick up the crab by the broadest part of the central body – the carapace.

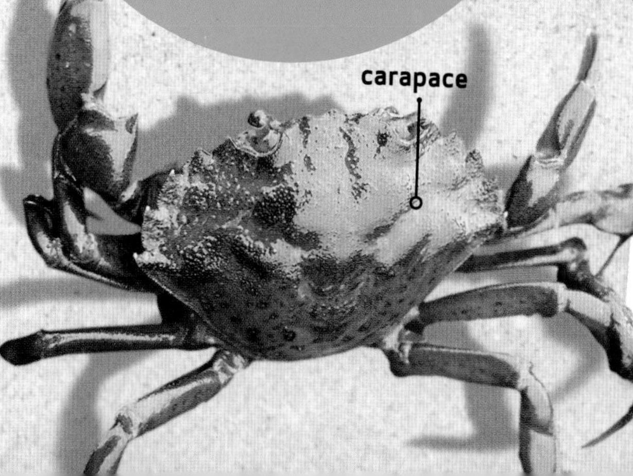

Crabbing

Crabbing over a harbour wall or dock is a great way to learn about crabs. It requires very little equipment and does not cause the crabs harm, when done properly.

Seashore safety

- Keep away from the water's edge.
- Go crabbing with an adult.
- Wash your hands with soap afterwards.
- Take your rubbish and equipment home with you.

You will need:

- a length of long string
- bait, such as a small piece of bacon

Tying bait onto a crab hook.

What to do:

- fill a bucket with fresh seawater;
- securely tie the bait to the string (a net can also be used);
- lower the string in to the water and let it hit the sea bottom;
- wait until you see or feel crabs tugging at the string;
- gently raise the string with crab attached to the bait and lower carefully into the bucket.

Find a crabbing spot that's out of the wind.

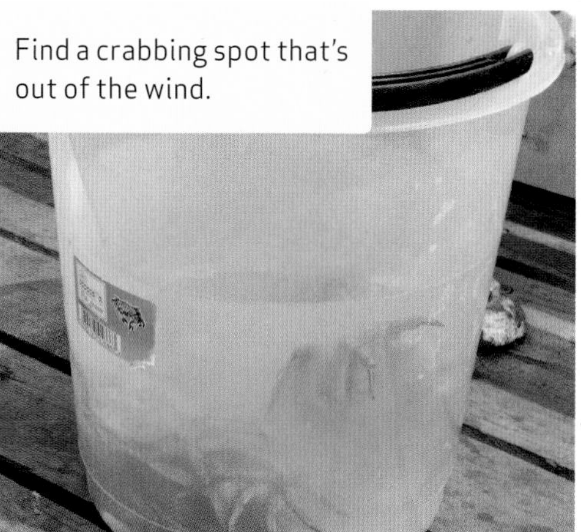

Keeping the crabs

- keep a few crabs in one bucket of fresh seawater;
- move your bucket out of the sun;
- observe the crabs in the bucket for a maximum time of 10 minutes;
- remove any crabs that are fighting (males are usually more aggressive);
- carefully return the crabs to the sea.

Tell your friends

Once you've been crabbing, teach your friends:

- how to pick up a crab properly (see page 79);
- how to tell the difference between a male and a female crab;
- how crabs moult.

Share everything you know about crabs!

Lobsters

Lobsters are ten-legged crustaceans with long bodies and tails. Young lobsters can be found in pools at low tide, while adult lobsters usually live in deeper water. Lobsters have poor sight, and use their antennae to taste and feel their environment.

A young diver gets up close to an American lobster.

Did you know?

As well as being able to walk, lobsters can swim backwards for short distances.

Five fascinating lobster facts

1 Scientists believe that lobsters can live for over 100 years.

2 Lobster blood is clear until it is exposed to air, when it turns blue.

3 Lobsters' front legs have hairs that can taste food in the water.

4 Teeth-like structures inside the lobster's stomach grind its food.

5 Lobsters pee from glands located near their antennae!

A rare bright blue lobster.

Lobster shells

Lobsters have a hard shell or **exoskeleton**, which must be shed to grow. The lobster swells with water, the shell cracks down the middle, and the lobster crawls out of its old shell. The skin then hardens to form a new, hard shell. Lobsters eat their old shell, which contains calcium that helps them grow.

A European common lobster.

A Californian lobster, moulting its old shell.

Common lobster

The common lobster in European waters is usually blue, while the American common lobster is often bluey-green with red claws. The pincers of the common lobster are different sizes: the larger one is used for crushing, while the smaller pincer cuts prey.

The two large antennae are used for fighting and defence against predators.

Spiny lobster

You can tell spiny lobsters apart from other 'true' lobster species by their long antennae and lack of large front claws. They use two smaller antennules to 'taste' the water, and find their way by detecting the Earth's magnetic field. Spiny lobsters can be found in almost all warm seas around the world.

Starfish

A symmetrical five-armed starfish

Did you know that starfish are not in fact fish at all? Starfish, or sea stars, belong to a group of creatures called **echinoderms**, which means 'spiny-skinned'. They can be found on seashores around the world, and are often symmetrical.

Look for sea stars in tidal pools.

Common starfish

These sea stars are commonly found at low tide in pools on the coast of the east Atlantic from Norway through to Africa. They have five arms, are usually orange, and grow up to 30 cm across.

This seven-armed starfish is regenerating two of its arms.

Did you know?

Starfish have an amazing ability to regrow arms that may have been lost to predators.

Starfish strandings

Following storms with strong winds, beaches can become covered with stranded starfish. Recently scientists have discovered 'starballing,' where starfish roll along the seabed at speed with their arms curled. This may help explain how these slow-moving starfish reach the shore.

A crown-of-thorns starfish, feasting on coral.

Thousands of starfish are stranded following a storm.

Crown-of-thorns starfish

One of the largest sea star species, the crown-of-thorns starfish has venomous spines all over its upper surface and up to 23 arms. It is most common in Australia where it preys on coral polyps, causing damage to reefs. Warm sea temperatures and overfishing of their predators have seen numbers of these spiky carnivores increase.

Pacific blood star

This starfish is bony-looking and less fleshy than many starfish species. Brightly coloured, it is usually red, but purple blood stars can be found along America's west coast, from Alaska to California.

How starfish feed and move

While a starfish has no brain, it does have a nerve ring and nerves that run down the length of its arms. Starfish can move and have a strange way of feeding.

A starfish moving to find a safe pool of seawater.

Did you know?

If you take a starfish out of a tidal pool, it will dry out quickly. Return starfish to the sea as soon as possible.

Make sure any starfish you collect are kept moist.

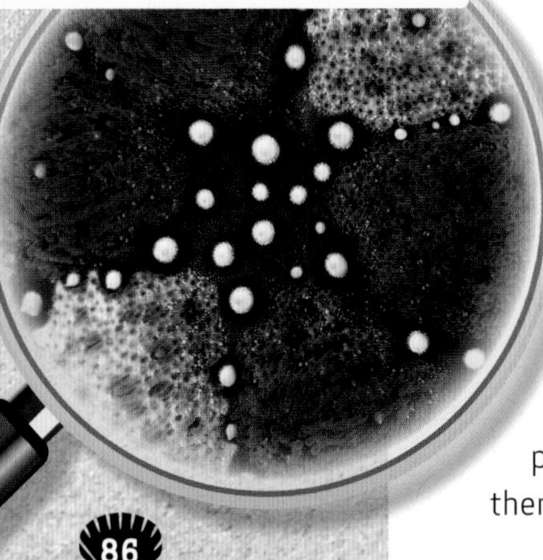

Starfish detect odours using receptors on their skin.

Sense of smell

Starfish have a highly developed sense of smell, and can detect the faint smell of their prey, as well as alerting them to nearby predators.

How do starfish move?

Starfish have grooves running on the underside of their arms, which have lots of tiny tube feet. The tube feet work together to move forwards. The common starfish moves slowly, at no more than 26 inches a minute.

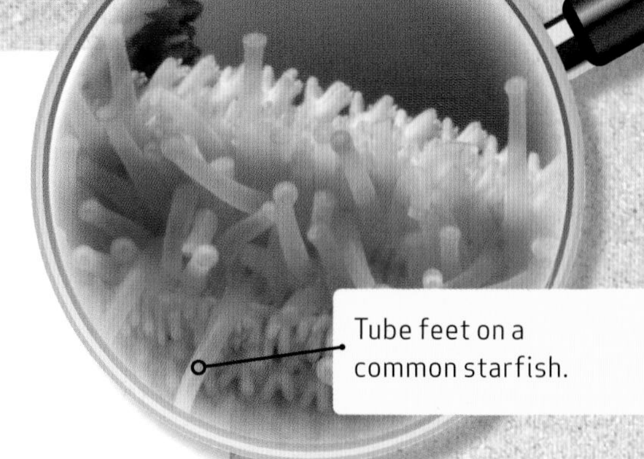

Tube feet on a common starfish.

Starfish madreporite

Starfish have a small spot on their upper surface called a madreporite. This sieve-like spot allows water in, which gives the starfish support and fills the tube feet to help it to move.

Starfish use their tube feet to open mussel shells.

Starfish feeding

Larger starfish will eat shellfish including mussels. They take hold of a shell using the tube feet on their arms, before prising it apart. A starfish then pushes one of its two stomachs out of its mouth and into the prey's shell. When the prey has been devoured, the starfish pulls its stomach back into its mouth. A special **enzyme** is released to help digest the flesh.

Sea urchins

Sea urchins can be found all over the world. These usually round, spiky creatures also include the flattened and hairy-looking heart urchins.

Common sea urchin

The common urchin is a large round urchin, although the shallower species are more flattened. It can be found across northwest Europe. The roe (or eggs) are eaten in many parts of Europe.

Edible sea urchins have large, round bodies and live in deeper waters.

A sea urchin test?

The sea urchin test is not a quiz, but the round skeleton that remains once the urchin has died. If you hold an urchin test to the light, you will see holes where the tube feet emerged to move just like a starfish.

An urchin test sits on the seabed.

A bright red slate-pencil urchin in Hawaiian waters.

Did you know?

Sea urchins also have stalked tiny biting and snapping attachments or **pedicellariae** that look like tube feet. They are used to deter predators, and some urchins even have venomous pedicellariae.

Slate-pencil sea urchin

The slate-pencil sea urchin has three types of spines: thick, triangular-shaped red spines that deter predators, shorter, flatter spines to clamp onto reeds and blunt, flat spines, which protect its body. It is most common on Hawaiian coral reefs.

The fire urchin has venomous pedicellariae.

Long-spined sea urchin

This urchin, as its name suggests, has very long spines of up to 12 cm in length. They are dark black and can be found in both the east and west of the Atlantic ocean. These urchins feed on algae, helping to stop overgrowth, which in turn helps keep coral reefs diverse and rich in life.

The long-spined urchin plays a big part in keeping coral reefs healthy.

How do sea urchins feed?

Sea urchins' mouths are on the underside of their body. Here, you can see the tips of five teeth, which open and close to scrape algae from the rocks.

A sea urchin's teeth are even sharper than its spines.

Did you know?

Sea urchin teeth stay sharp despite scraping on hard rocks as they self-sharpen. Scientists are studying this action to help them make self-sharpening tools.

Sea urchin teeth

The teeth of urchins are constantly growing. They self-sharpen because of the way crystals in the teeth are arranged in layers. The teeth break along these layers, leaving a sharp new edge.

Urchin teeth can chew through rock without becoming blunt.

An urchin's amazing Aristotle's lantern.

Aristotle's lantern

The mouth of most sea urchins is made up of five teeth, which stick out of a chewing organ known as Aristotle's lantern. Sixty different muscles work together to perfom a strong biting action.

Predators of the red sea urchin include sea otters, some birds and humans.

Sea urchin survival

Some urchins can live up to an incredible 200 years. They suffer little disease, but are sometimes eaten by predators or are harvested by fishermen.

Seashore fish

Hundreds of fish species live on the seashore between the tides, in pools and even in rocky crevices. They can be found guarding eggs that are attached to rocks.

The clingfish, on egg-guarding duty.

Protective parents

For many seashore fish species, it is the male that has the job of fiercely guarding the eggs laid by the female. Some fish, such as the clingfish, have suckers on their underside to help them stay in place on the rocks and protect their eggs from predators.

Did you know?

As with their close relatives, seahorses, it is the male pipefish that becomes pregnant. He will hold the eggs in his brood pouch until they are ready to be released as mini versions of the parents.

Common blenny

Like all blennies, this seashore fish has a long fin that runs down the length of its back. Blennies have big eyes and a grumpy-looking face, which can be seen peering out from rocky holes. They can survive periods out of water by absorbing oxygen through their skin, which has no scales.

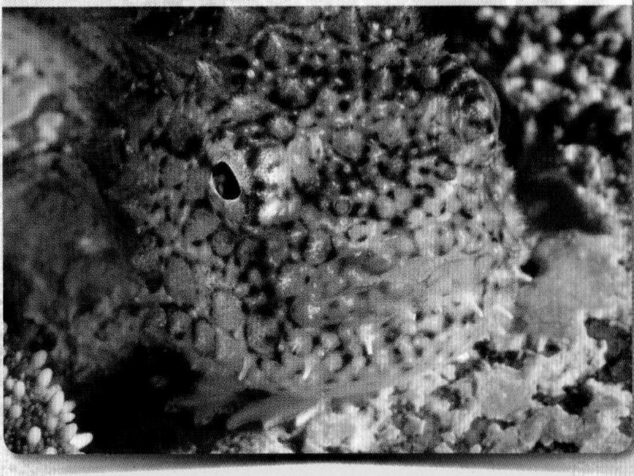

An Atlantic spiny lumpsucker.

Lumpsuckers

Lumpsuckers are prehistoric, chubby-looking fish. They will swim into shallower waters to breed. While young, they will use their sucker to remain in the shallows. Male lumpsuckers also guard their brood of eggs.

A common blenny guards eggs on the rocks at low tide.

A worm pipefish.

Worm pipefish

Pipefish are also related to the seahorse. They have a large snout for sucking in prey from the water and a long tail. Found between the tides on the seashore, this species is well camouflaged among seaweed.

Egg-case hunt

While sightings of sharks or rays from the seashore are rare, seashore watchers are likely to have come across the eggs from some species washed up on beaches. These egg capsules are commonly called **'mermaids' purses'.**

The egg case of a greater spotted catshark.

Egg-laying sharks and rays

Sharks and rays that lay eggs are called 'oviparous'. It is thought that about one third of shark species lay eggs that hatch outside the body.

Shark egg cases, such as this one, contain a single egg.

Mermaids' purse facts

- The leathery outer layer of a mermaids' purse is made from a substance similar to human nails.
- Mermaids' purse eggs can be identified by their size, shape and tendrils
- Tendrils on the purses help the egg attach to seaweed so that the egg can stay in the water.
- Just like a chicken egg, there is a large yolk, on which the young shark feeds.
- As the yolk gets smaller and the shark becomes more mature, it will nuzzle its way out of the purse.

Catshark eggs, attached to coral.

Treasure trail

In some countries, egg-case findings are reported to shark scientists. This helps scientists learn where and how many eggs are being laid each year. Head down to the seashore after heavy storms to see if you can find any empty mermaids' purses washed ashore. If you can, report your findings to a local shark group.

The Port Jackson spiral egg case.

A mermaid's purse with curly tendrils.

Extraordinary eggs

The Port Jackson and horn sharks of Australian waters lay egg cases shaped like a corkscrew.

Seashore wildlife

The seashore is a fantastic place to discover wildlife, and not just in rock pools. From some coastlines you may also spot larger mammals, fish and birds.

Even large whales can be seen from the seashore.

Binoculars

Binoculars help you see wildlife much closer, without scaring it away. Wearing binoculars all the time, though, will mean you may miss things and get tired eyes.

Use binoculars to observe stationary or faraway wildlife.

Wildlife-watching tips

Using a camera will help you identify creatures later. You may see more wildlife on calm days. Look out for:

- unusual patterns on the sea's surface;
- frenzied feeding activity from birds;
- ripples in the sea from diving whales;
- **dorsal** fins in the waves;
- sprays of water.

Try using a seashore telescope to search for wildlife.

Did you know?

Some sea birds can be identified from their flight pattern. Some stay very close to the water, while others soar much higher.

When to watch wildlife ?

You may find certain times are better than others for particular feeding habits or behaviour. Head to your beach and learn the patterns of the larger wildlife.

Get to know your local whale- or dolphin-watching spots.

The Manx shearwater skims the surface of the sea in calm conditions.

Seashore safety

- Give large wildlife plenty of space.
- Take care not to disturb animals during breeding time, or when caring for their young.

Sea birds

Sea birds have evolved to be able to successfully live on the coast and out at sea, feeding in seawater. Sea birds guide sailors to land, fishermen to fish and are a treat for seashore watchers to observe.

A gull searches for food among the rubbish.

Sea birds and plastic

Sadly, some birds will mistake plastic for food. Once swallowed, their stomachs become filled with plastic, which can lead to dehydration and death.

Did you know?

Sea birds have a special salt gland above their eyes that allows them to drink saltwater. The excess salt is then 'sneezed' out through nostrils in the bill.

Terns

Terns are **migratory** birds that are found all over the world. They usually breed in large colonies and lay their eggs on bare ground, while the white fairy tern rather riskily lays its egg on a branch.

A nesting white fairy tern.

The herring gull gets rid of excess salt through its bill.

A black-backed gull makes a meal of a washed-up seal.

Gulls

Gulls are fairly large sea birds, with the great black-backed gull being the largest. Gulls are **scavengers** and eat live food, too. They are such unfussy eaters that they can even be spotted eating chips in seaside resorts.

Puffin

There are three main types of Puffin: the Atlantic, the horned and the tufted. These small birds have impressive, coloured beaks when they're breeding. A puffin's beak usually holds around ten fish at a time, and they have short wings that allow them to swim underwater.

Dolphins and porpoises

Dolphins and porpoises can be spotted from some seashores. They are marine air-breathing mammals that give birth to live young and produce milk. Dolphins usually have a beak and cone-shaped teeth, while porpoises are beakless and have flattened, spade-shaped teeth.

Bottlenose dolphin

The bottlenose dolphin can be found in all our oceans. It is the most recognised type of dolphin and has strong relationships with members of its pod. Large and acrobatic, this dolphin has no obvious patterns on its body.

Bottlenose dolphins can be seen from the seashore, surfing the waves.

Spinner dolphin

The spinner dolphin is found in warmer oceans. As the name suggests, this species twists and spins its streamlined body in the water. They often play close to the shore and around boats.

Echolocation

Dolphins see, find food and navigate using sound. They produce high-frequency clicks or sounds, which bounce off objects in the sea around them. The echoes of the sound travel back to the dolphin's jaw and a jelly-filled 'melon' and then on to the brain where they interpret and 'see' the sounds.

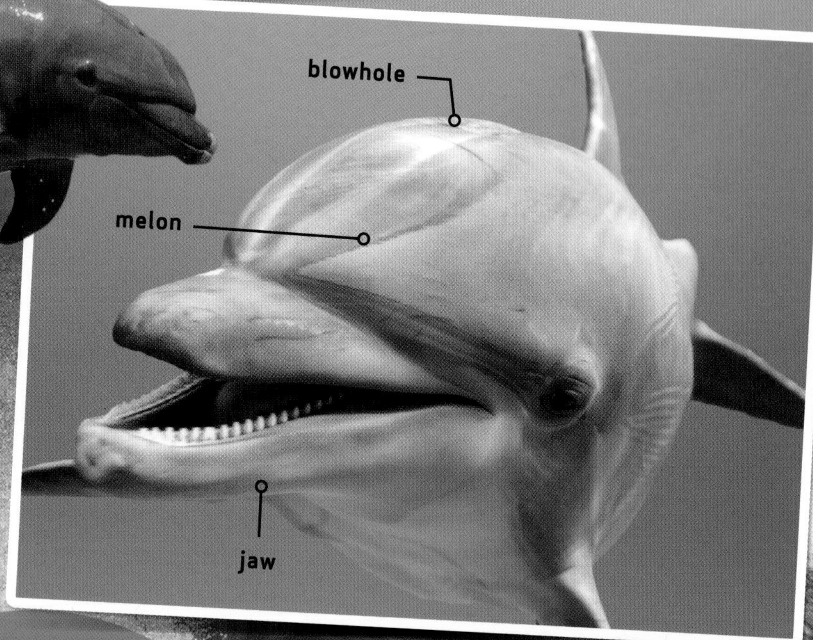

Harbour porpoise

The harbour porpoise is found in shallow waters in the North Atlantic and Pacific oceans. It is relatively small and chunky with a very small dorsal fin, which can be seen in calm seas close to the shore.

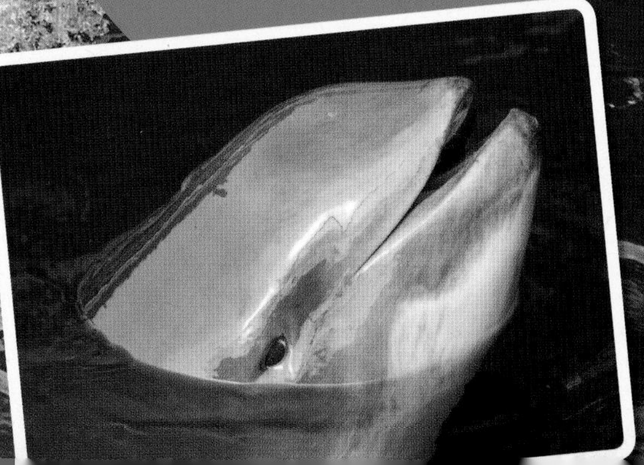

Did you know?

Killer whales and pilot whales are not whales at all but beakless dolphins.

Whales

Whales have evolved from land-living mammals, but now live, breed and feed underwater. They have thick blubber to keep them warm and use blowholes to breathe. There are two main types of whales – toothed whales and baleen whales.

Baleen and toothed whales

Baleen whales, like humpbacks, have two blowholes on the top of their body and no teeth. Bristly **baleen plates** in the whale's jaw act like a sieve to strain huge volumes of water, leaving food such as krill, crustaceans and small fish.

Toothed whales, like sperm whales, have teeth to capture their prey, and only one blowhole. They rely on sonar to find their way around the ocean and their food.

Humpback whales, showing their baleen plates while feeding.

Right whales

Right whales are types of baleen whales. There is a northern and southern species. They are recognisable by their V-shaped snout and lack of dorsal fin. They will come in to shallower waters to give birth every three to four years.

The southern right whale.

How do whales breathe?

Like all mammals, whales require air to breathe. They must come to the surface of the ocean to take in oxygen. When surfacing, they forcefully exhale air from the blowhole, before rapidly breathing in large amounts of oxygen (twice as much as we can store) in their blood. This allows the whale to dive for long periods.

Humpback whale

Humpback whales can sometimes be seen from the shore, **bubble-net feeding** or performing displays of flipper-slapping acrobatics. Humpbacks have long wing-like flippers with white undersides, and can be found worldwide.

The minke whale.

Minke whale

The minke whale can be found in the northern hemisphere. This pecies has an obvious white band on its ippers and a tall dorsal fin. Minke can e seen feeding among sea birds, often turning on their side to **lunge-feed**.

Sharks

Sharks have lived on Earth for millions of years – even before dinosaurs existed. They can swim in the deepest oceans and in waters as shallow as 30 cm and there are over 400 different species worldwide. Sharks help keep reefs healthy by keeping fish populations in check.

The great white is one of the fiercest shark species

Dangerous predators?

Sharks have a reputation as fearsome predators, but the chances of being injured or killed by one are incredibly small. Only a very few species ever attack humans – the rest are completely harmless.

Certain beaches in Florida, Hawaii, South Africa and Australia are hotspots for shark sightings.

Shark hunting

Humans kill sharks for food and also for sport. Shark's-fin soup and shark meat are eaten in many countries. It is thought that 100 million sharks are killed each year, often just for their fins. This has led to a huge drop in shark numbers.

Shark fins drying, to be made into soup.

Tiger shark

Tiger sharks get their name thanks to the vertical stripes found on young sharks. The marks fade as the shark reaches adulthood. Tiger sharks have sharp, serrated teeth and jaws that are powerful enough to crack open the shells of clams and sea turtles.

Tiger sharks are under threat due to **finning**.

Did you know?

Sharks have an organ called the **ampullae of Lorenzini**, which they use to sense the electrical field coming from their prey.

The great hammerhead's favourite prey is stingray.

Hammerhead shark

With its mallet-shaped head and eyes set wide apart, the hammerhead can detect prey more easily than other sharks. Nine different species of hammerhead can be found in tropical waters in Africa, America and Australia.

ampullae

The shark's electrical-detecting pores are found close to their mouths.

A Mediterrean monk seal.

Seals

Seals are strong and efficient swimmers that can forage far out to sea. They haul themselves onto land to give birth, moult and escape from predators. While sea lions and fur seals have ear flaps, 'true' seals do not.

Mediterranean monk seal

This rare seal has an 'endangered' conservation status. They can be found in the Mediterranean and off the coastal waters of Northwest Africa. They are brown on their backs with paler bellies. Fewer than 600 seals still exist.

The harbour or common seal.

Harbour or common seal

The harbour seal has more of a rounded, dog-like face with V-shaped nostrils. They are common to the shores of North America, northwest Europe and the western Pacific. Pups are well-adapted to start swimming soon after birth.

A gray seal and her pup.

Grey seal

The grey seal has a long, sloping, flat muzzle with parallel nostrils. These grey-brown patchy seals can be found in Northern Europe and northeast Canada. The male bull is noticeably larger than the female, and their pups have soft, white fur.

Seals have been on the Earth for more than 15 million years.

Did you know?

Seals are thought to have evolved from bears or otter-like land creatures.

A grey seal strikes a banana pose.

Banana pose

When on land, some seals lie in a typical banana pose. They keep their head and flippers (which have no thick fat) high off the ground to keep themselves dry and warm.

How do seals dive?

Seals have incredible ability and agility underwater. They can dive to great depths for long periods of time to catch their prey, which includes fish, squid and octopus.

An agile Atlantic grey seal.

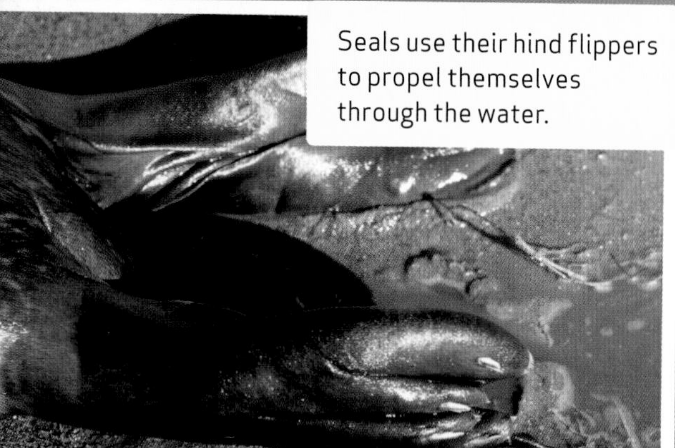
Seals use their hind flippers to propel themselves through the water.

Seals swimming

Seals use their fore flippers to help them steer in the water, and hold them to their side when they are swimming at speed. Their hind flippers propel them through the water as their body moves from side to side through the water.

Did you know?

The Weddell seal can swim underwater for up to 45 minutes, and to depths of over 600 metres.

Weddell seals spend much of their time below the Antarctic ice.

How can seals dive for so long?

Seals and mammals need oxygen to survive underwater. The seal's body is adapted to dive for long periods by:

- being very streamlined;
- swimming in a way that is efficient and uses less oxygen;
- reducing their heart rates;
- restricting blood flow to non-essential body parts;
- having lots of blood to store oxygen;
- having lots of **haemoglobin** in the blood that carries the oxygen;
- being able to cope with low levels of oxygen in the blood.

Seals restrict blood flow to their vital organs for longer dives.

Underwater pressure

As you dive deeper underwater the pressure becomes greater. Blubber, a layer of fat under the seal's skin, does not compress under this pressure. Seals are also able to remove air from their lungs so that damaging nitrogen can't absorb into their bodies and make them ill.

Seals are master divers.

Human divers

Human scuba divers need lots of equipment to dive to relatively shallow depths. Compressed air in a tank, insulating suits, masks to see, weights to sink and inflatable jackets to help them return to the sea's surface safely are all essential pieces of kit.

Notes for parents and teachers

- Get to know your local beach, and become aware of any safety issues. Consider mobile phone reception or closest telephone box, and availability of lifeguards, toilets and cafés.

- Make sure children are dressed in suitable clothing for different weather conditions. Sturdy footwear that they can get wet is essential, as is protection from the sun, cold and heat.

DANGEROUS CLIFFS KEEP OFF

- Give a health and safety briefing at the beginning of a session. This can be made more interactive by asking children about potential hazards. They may suggest slippery rocks, the weather, the tide and running water.

- Learn with your children. Take seashore guides, photographs and make notes to help identify a creature later.

- Encourage children to question what they see. Even if you may not have the answers there and then, research the answers when you return to school or at home.

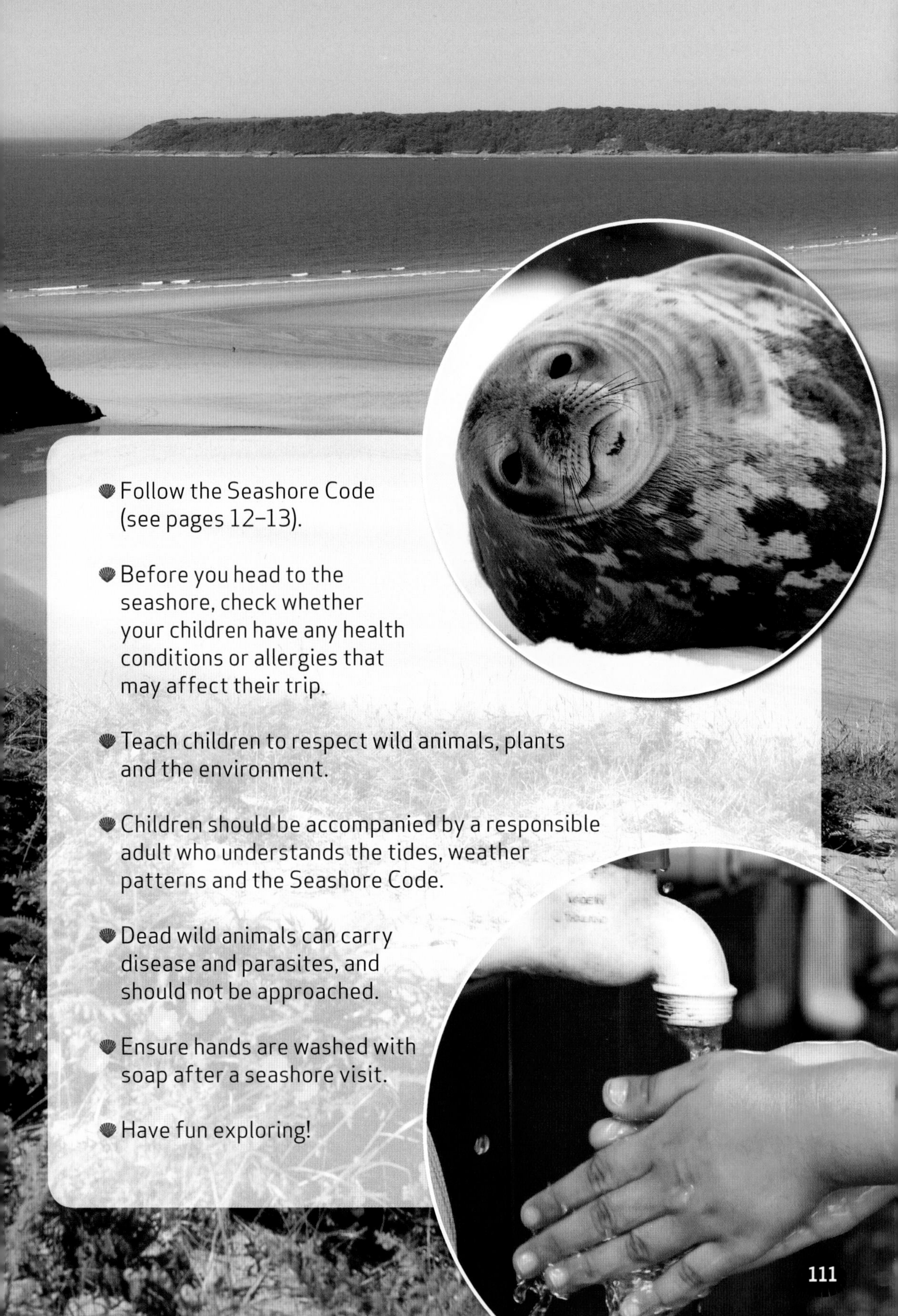

- Follow the Seashore Code (see pages 12–13).
- Before you head to the seashore, check whether your children have any health conditions or allergies that may affect their trip.
- Teach children to respect wild animals, plants and the environment.
- Children should be accompanied by a responsible adult who understands the tides, weather patterns and the Seashore Code.
- Dead wild animals can carry disease and parasites, and should not be approached.
- Ensure hands are washed with soap after a seashore visit.
- Have fun exploring!

Glossary

algae	Marine plants, including seaweeds.
ampullae of Lorenzini	The organ sharks use to sense the electrical field coming from their prey.
anemone	A marine creature with stinging tentacles that lives on rocks.
baleen plate	The strong, bendy plate that a whale uses to filter its prey from the seawater.
bivalve	A mollusc that has a hinged pair of shells.
bloom	A large group of jellyfish.
bubble-net feeding	A technique used by humpback whales to catch fish by blowing bubbles below them, forcing them upwards.
cirri	The curled legs of a barnacle.
climate	The weather conditions in an area over time.
cnidaria	The group of marine animals that includes jellyfish.
cnidocytes	The stinging cells of anemones, jellyfish and corals.
corals	Sea animals that stay in one place throughout their adult lives. Together, corals form a coral reef.
crustacean	The group of creatures which includes crabs, lobster, shrimp and barnacles.
cyprid	The larvae at the second larval stage of a barnacle or crustacean.
dorsal	A fin (or fins) located on the upper part or back of a fish, whale, dolphin or porpoise.
echinoderms	Spiny starfish, sea urchins and sea cucumbers.

echolocation The production of sound used for communication, navigation and locating prey.

endangered Seriously at risk of becoming extinct.

enzyme A protein that speeds up a chemical reaction, such as digestion.

erosion The gradual wearing away by pebbles, sand, water or wind.

estuary A body of water where a river meets the sea.

exoskeleton The external, hard covering of creatures like crabs.

fauna Animals that belong to a particular region or habitat, such as the seashore.

flora The plants that belong to a particular region.

fluorescence Giving off light or glowing extremely bright colours.

frond The part of seaweed that looks like a leaf.

gastropod Molluscs like snails and slugs, often with a single shell.

ghost nets Fishing nets lost at sea that continue to catch fish or marine creatures.

haemoglobin A protein of red blood cells that contains iron and carries oxygen from the lungs to the tissues.

holdfast The part of seaweed attached to rocks or surfaces.

hypothermia A low body temperature, which may be caused by being exposed to cold weather.

lunge-feed When a whale spectacularly lunges at its prey, often at high speed, to capture large amounts of prey.

madreporite An echinoderm's sieve plate that draws in seawater to help the creature to move.

mermaids' purse The leathery egg case of fish such as shark or skate.

mermaids' tears Small pieces of plastic or glass that are found in the world's oceans.

migratory An animal that moves from one region or habitat to another according to the seasons.

mollusc The group of animals that includes snails, slugs, mussels, octopus and squid.

moult When a marine animal sheds its shell.

nauplius The larvae at the first larval stage of a barnacle or crustacean.

neap tides A tide in which the difference between high and low tide is the least. They occur around the quarter moons.

nurdles Small plastic pellets that get moulded into larger plastic objects.

ovary The organ where eggs are produced.

oviparous Where eggs are produced and hatched outside the body.

pedicellariae An echinoderm's tiny pincers.

photosynthesis The process of using sunlight to make nutrients or energy from carbon dioxide and water, while producing oxygen.

photosynthesize To produce energy by photosynthesis.

phytoplankton Microscopic plankton that photosynthesize.

plankton Mostly very small organisms that drift in the ocean.

polyps	The body of a single coral or sea anemone.
predator	An animal that hunts a smaller, weaker creature for food, such as a shark eating a fish or crab.
radula	A tongue-like structure used to scrape food from surfaces.
sailor's valentine	A souvenir made from shells, often brought home as a gift from a sailor's voyage in Victorian times.
scavenger	An animal that feeds on dead animal or plant material, or rubbish.
shingle	A shingle beach is made up of small pebbles rather than sand.
sonar	Sonar is short for sound navigation and ranging. It is a way to find objects (such as prey) underwater by sending and reflecting sound waves.
spat	A bivalve larva that has attached to a surface.
spring tides	The very high and very low tides which occur around a full and new moon.
stipe	The stalk on a seaweed.
strandline	The mark left by the high tide, often made up of seaweed and other washed-up objects.
tentacles	A sea creature's long, thin limbs, used for moving, sensing or catching food.
upwellings	When deep, cold water rises to the surface.
zones	The different areas of the seashore from the lower zone to the splash zone.
zooxanthellae	An algae that lives in coral and uses photosynthesis to make energy.

Index

Picture credits

Key: t = top, b = bottom, r = right, l = left, c = centre, bg = background.

Alamy: 11b Suretha Rous; 15c Neil Foster; 18b & 110b Nik Taylor; 23t Paulo Oliveira; 26–27bg Gary K Smith; 27c & 92c FLPA; 27b Nature Photographers Ltd; 37c Ross Armstrong; 38t Plrang GFX; 53c WaterFrame; 54t, 55c & 95c Minden Pictures; 62t & 67c blickwinkel; 62b Nature Photographers Ltd; 66cl Ian Redding; 66b Steve Taylor ARPS; 67t age fotostock; 68t Marcos Veiga; 68b Natural Visions; 69t Steve Trewhella; 69b Bill Coster; 71t Mark Boulton; 71c Jim Kidd; 71b INTERFOTO; 72t, 75b & 82t Jeff Rotman; 72b, 73t, 73b, 86bl & 108t Nature Picture Library; 80t keith morris; 81t veryan dale; 81c D Hale-Sutton; 84t Aqua Image; 86br RFStock; 87t Robert HENNO; 87c Tim Gainey; 87b age fotostock; 93t Robert La Salle/Aqua-Photo; 93b WATER RIGHTS; 96t Ian Lamond; 97c Chris Gomersall; 97b Johnny Habbell; 98b Jens Metschurat; 100b age fotostock; 101bl Arterra Picture Library; 107b Arterra Picture Library; 108c Juniors Bildarchiv GmbH; 109b imageBROKER. **Chris Howarth:** 32–33bg; 33c. **Cumbria Wildlife Trust and Ellie Chaney:** 29t. **Dana Behnke:** 39t. **Frank Rocco © WashedAshore.org:** 28t; 28–29b. **Getty Images:** 6b Michael Grimm; 6–7bg, 10b Jerry Monkman; 10–11bg, 42–43bg & 68–69bg Sebastian Schollmeyer/EyeEm; 12bl Shestock; 21b Klaus Vedfelt; 65b vernonwiley; 75t Hiroya Minakuchi/Minden Pictures; 75b Daniel Gotshall; 77bl Barrie Watts; 77br Steve Head/EyeEm; 76l Karen Gowlett-Holmes; 76tc Oxford Scientific; 76b Robert F. Sisson; 80b Carol Anne Williams/EyeEm; 94t Paul Kay; 99b Rodger Shagam; 102t Mark Carwardine; **John Turnbull:** 67b. **Maya Plass:** 6t; 6c; 6–7t; 9b; 12br; 12–13bg; 19b; 19c; 22b; 24t; 24b; 25b; 33t; 34t; 34l; 39c; 42t; 42b; 43t; 42b; 44b; 46t; 46bl; 46br; 47; 48t; 48b; 49t; 50t; 50b; 51t; 51b; 52t; 52b; 53b; 56t; 59t; 63t; 63b; 78t; 78rc; 79b; 84c; 84b; 88t; 89t; 90t; 90b. **Dr Richard Kirby:** 40b; 41t; 42t. **Science Photo Library:** 76cr Wim van Egmond. **SeaPics:** 37t; 82b, 83c. **Shutterstock:** 1 & 30t Jethita; 2–3 Irina Mos; 3c Elena Schweitzer; 4–5 Disavorabuth; 6–7b Sheila Fitzgerald; 8t turtix; 8b Jen Petrie; 8–9bg, 60–61bg & 116–119bg Jacek Fulawka; 9t Brian A Jackson; 10t Stephen Marques; 10–11b Melinda Fawver; 11t & 110t; Youproduction; 13t & 110c Wil Tilroe-Otte; 13b Gail Johnson; 13c Maciej Bledowski; 14–15bg Jonathan Lingel; 14t, 45c, 57t, 58t & 85t Ethan Daniels; 14c Peter Titmuss; 15bl Daniel Hussey; 15br Vlad G; 16bl Helen Hotson; 16br EpicStockMedia;16–17t Miami2you; 16–17bg Savvapanf Photo; 17c Henner Damke; 17b Dmitry Rukhlenko; 18–19bg B Calkins; 19t Aleks Melnik; 20–21bg Mike Charles; 20b Corepics VOF; 21t moprea; 21c Monkey Business Images; 22bg Africa Studio; 22t Asia Images; 23b Doug McLean; 24–25bg, 36–37bg, 72–73bg, 76–77bg, 78–79bg, 84–85bg & 86–87bg wandee007; 24t EvrenKalinbacak; 25t Porridge Picture Library; 26t Dennis Jacobsen; 26b Cardinal Arrows; 27t Naaman Abreu; 28t Gearstd; Vadarshop 28b; 30–31 bg B Calkins; 30b Ingrid Balabanova; 31t & 37b Laura Dinraths; 31c Aneta Waberska; 31b Melanie Hobson; 33b Davdeka; 34–35bg Preto Perola; 34c & 52–53bg Helen Hotson; 35b ElenVD; 36b Petr Malyshev; 36t Joy Prescott; 38b & 64–65bg BlueOrange Studio; 38–39bg & 94–95bg sergeisimonov; 39b Dutourdumonde Photography; 40–41bg borzywoj; 40bl Vitaly Korovin; 40t Rattiya Thongdumhyu; 44–45bg & 61b Richard Carey; 45t Dan Bagur; 45b TasfotoNL; 46–47bg siro46; 48–49bg divedog; 49b Kampol Taepanich; 50–51bg hasrullnizam; 53t mikeledray; 54–55bg Shvaygert Ekaterina; 54b littlesam; 55t ECOSTOCK; 55b Peter Leahy; 56–57bg & 61t Rich Carey; 56c ChameleonsEye; 57b JC Photo; 58–59bg & 82–83 bg rangizz; 58t saraporn; 58c MattiaATH; 58b Chris Troch; 60t borzywoj; 60b Yuri Megel; 61t Business stock; 62–63bg PRILL; 63c DJ Mattaar; 64t Mike Laptev; 66–67bg & 92–93bg; sixninepixels; 66t Lizard; 66cr Bildagentur Zoonar GmbH; 70–71bg holbox; 70b kaband; 74–74bg & 114–119bg sit; 74t Alfonso de Tomas; 74b carekung; 78b davemhuntphotography; 78t Sapnocte; 79t Kelvin Wong; 83t davidpstephens; 83b Palo_ok; 85t Schippers; 85b Randimal; 86t Brian Maudsley; 88–89bg & 108–109bg Andrey_Kuzmin; 88b Bjoern Wylezich; 89b SUPHANAT KHUMSAP; 89c bearacreative; 90–91bg, 104–105bg & 106–107bg Benny Marty; 91b Joe Belanger; 92t Seaphotoart; 92b & 105br Yann Hupert; 95t, 101t & 107c Andrea Izzotti; 96–97bg Bellamaree; 96t Dai Mar Tamarack; 96b Pavel Semenov; 98–99bg Images by Lisa; 98t LouieLea; 99tl Alan Tunnicliffe; 99tr 18042011; 100–101bg Willyam Bradberry; 101br Xavier MARCHANT; 102b Shane Gross; 103t Tim Robinson; 103cr Jo Crebbin; 103cl Joanne Weston; 103br & 105bl Martin Prochazkacz; 104t Jim Agronick; 104b hidesy; 105t Lano Lan; 105cr Fiona Ayerst; 106b Pat Stornebrink; 106t zaferkizilkaya; 107b Frank Fichtmueller; 108b & 111t Mogens Trolle; 109t Valerijs Novickis; 110–111bg Mike Charles; 111b Thanamat Somwan.